TALES FROM
A CIVIL WAR PLANTATION:
∞CREEKSIDE∞

by

Louisa Emmons

Cover Photograph: "Creekside" by Laura Smith Shuler.

Hollow Tree Press
P.O. Box 322
Morganton, NC 28680

ISBN-13: 978-0692323021
ISBN-10: 0692323023

PREFACE

My memories of childhood are abundant with adventures experienced in and around Creekside. My sister, Mary, and I spent many happy hours playing in the places noted in this book without ever dreaming I would one day take a deeper interest in their origins.

The "clubs" of our childhood were held in the cellar where a beloved family servant, "Aunt" Harriett once lived. Time was spent climbing the stairs and sliding down the banister. These same steps had once been trod upon by Union General Gillem and the men of an invading army who headquartered at Creekside. We played in the cool, green ivy of the ice house and climbed the magnolia tree. A Union camp bed, left behind during the Civil War, became the garden bench that we sat on. We laughed at old family pictures, particularly at the one of Louisa Anne Patton with her flat hairdo which led the children of the family to nickname her "Flat Top." I would learn later that she was the grandmother of my grandmother who had inherited her name, and that I, in turn, had been given that name. In later years, I would venture down into the potato hole with friends in high school who were eager to find another Yankee button like the one my uncle once found there. My sister, who was always braver than I, once climbed out on the roof and dared me to challenge her to walk across the roof to the far chimney. She did so without even waiting for my reply. I would later learn that the same back wing of the house had been built atop the pre-Revolutionary War foundation of another plantation. History was everywhere.

Needless to say, my greatest interest in Civil War history, Burke County history, and family history has always been the wonderful tales of real people. I have tried to uncover as many of these stories as possible in order to preserve them. A few stories are fairly well known, because my great great grandfather, Colonel Thomas George Walton, related them long ago in his writings; most of the stories in this book are known only to my family. Many of the stories are told by family members themselves through their letters and their private papers.

Because all stories exist within a context, I have attempted to ground these tales within the framework of their time, which in most cases is the Civil War.

I have included photographs and documents, and I have transcribed the words of those who are long gone. Some of the stories are humorous, while others are tales of grief and struggle. The journey has been a very personal one for me.

For those whose interest is genealogical, I have appended a portion of the family tree to the end of this book which traces the line from which Colonel Thomas George Walton descended. I have traced from the first of our Walton kin who emigrated from Walton-on-Thames in Surrey County, England in the 1600s.

Louisa Emmons." Creekside," June 2013.

ACKNOWLEDGEMENTS

Those who deserve the greatest share of thanks in this endeavor are the ones who are the subjects of these pages, those I am unable to thank for their bravery and humor because they are no longer with us.

In particular, I would like to thank my grandmother, Louise Walton Boggs, now deceased, who loved writing about and sharing the tales and history of her beloved home, Creekside, and without whose written and spoken versions of these tales I could never have produced this book.

Many thanks go to my mother, Mary Alexander, who kindly provided me with resources and patiently recounted family stories to me.

To my husband, Kirk, and my son, Alex, who supported and encouraged me throughout this project, thank you for your love and patience.

Special thanks to my cousin Laura Smith Shuler and my son Alex Emmons whose expertise provided a number of photos in this book.

Thanks go to Gale Benfield, Curator of the North Carolina Room at the Burke County Public Library in Morganton, for assistance in finding North Carolina rosters of Confederate soldiers and for assisting me in acquiring permission to use historic photographs from the *Picture Burke Project*.

To the staff of Amherst County Museum and Historical Society in Amherst, Virginia, many thanks for assistance in finding genealogical information on the Waltons of Virginia.

To the people of Burke County, this history is your history because it is the story of our shared journey across time and part of the fabric of our community.

TABLE OF CONTENTS

I. THE WALTON FAMILY

George Walton (1749-1804), Signer of the
Declaration of Independence for the State of
Georgia. Photograph: Biographical Directory
of the United States Congress, U.S. Senate
Historical Office.

Willow Hill, near Canoe Creek in Burke County. Captain James Murphy and his wife, Margaret McDowell, occupied Willow Hill which was probably built by his father-in-law, Hugh McDowell (1742-1772). Murphy emigrated from Ireland and served with distinction in the American Revolution in the Battles of Cane Creek, Ramsour's Mill and King's Mountain. Murphy's granddaughter would marry Thomas George Walton in 1837. Photograph: Library of Congress.

1. THE LIFE OF A PLANTER: THOMAS GEORGE WALTON

One of Thomas George Walton's ancestors, his great uncle, was a signer of the Declaration of Independence. The signer, named George Walton, was born in Virginia in 1749 and later became a lifelong resident of Georgia. He was admitted to the bar in 1774 and served as a delegate to the Continental Congress in 1776. At 26 years of age, Walton was one of the youngest signers, and his was the last signature placed on the Declaration of Independence.

Walton was a colonel in the Continental Army when he was shot from his horse during the Battle of Savannah in 1778. He was hit in the knee by a cannonball and taken prisoner by the British. A year later he was exchanged for an imprisoned Captain of the Royal Navy.

During the Revolution, when men wore knee breeches, hose and buckle shoes, a famous portrait of the signers, dressed in the style of the day, was painted by John Trumbull in 1817. The painting was titled, *The Declaration of Independence*. John Randolph of Virginia, upon viewing the famous portrait of the signers, noted with amusement that George Walton had the finest legs in the delegation.

George Walton was a long-standing foe of Button Gwinnett, a representative of Georgia who served in the Continental Congress and who also signed the Declaration of Independence. Because of his keen dislike for Gwinnett, Walton played a role in the duel that took place between political enemies General Lachlan McIntosh and Button Gwinnett which led to Gwinnett's death. His involvement resulted in political censure by the state legislature for Walton. The scandal does not appear to have hurt Walton politically; in his lifetime he served twice as Governor of Georgia, then Chief Justice, then a superior court judge and, finally, a United States Senator. It was, however, a typical chapter in the colorful and controversial life led by George Walton.

Walton County in northern Georgia was named after George Walton. Interestingly, the creation of this county in 1803, a year before Walton's death, led to a "war" between North Carolina and Georgia known as the Walton War. A small strip of land called the "Orphan Strip" bordered North Carolina, South Carolina and Georgia. It was this piece of land which became Walton County, the creation of which became a source of bitter contention between two states, particularly with regard to who would pay taxes to whom. State boundaries were not clearly defined in the contested area, and while South Carolinians accepted the creation of Walton County by Georgia, North Carolinians did not.

Violent disputes erupted between citizens from North Carolina and Georgia, culminating in the death of a Buncombe County constable named John Havner who was killed when struck in the head by a musket. The government of Buncombe County called in the militia to arrest ten officials from Walton County and bring them to North Carolina for trial. The prisoners were brought to Morganton to await justice, but all ten of them escaped before being brought to trial. The scandal eroded the political power of Walton County and the state government of Georgia failed to defend the accused Walton County officials.

The issue was finally settled by disinterested parties from both Georgia and North Carolina who were called upon to resurvey the Orphan Strip. North Carolina was proclaimed the victor in the war, and the so-called Orphan Strip is now part of Transylvania County in western North Carolina. In spite of the resolution, Georgia refused to concede defeat until 1818 when it responded by carving out another Walton County within its boundaries.

◆ ◆ ◆

Thomas (nicknamed "Tammie") Walton (1782-1859), the father of Thomas George Walton, was born in Amherst County, Virginia, and moved with his family to Charleston, South Carolina, prior to 1790. He married Martha Matilda McEntire (1784-1868) in 1803, the daughter of innkeeper James McEntire and his wife Nancy Young. Born in Tyrone County, Ireland, her family moved first to Buncombe County, N.C. in 1785, and then to Burke County, N.C. in 1793. Interestingly, two of Thomas' brothers, William and George, would also marry daughters of James McEntire: William married Jennie McEntire and George married Nancy McEntire.

Thomas Walton became a successful businessman, involving himself in a number of business ventures. His brother William opened a general store and counting house in Morganton where Thomas served as a clerk and assayer, later purchasing the business from his brother. Gold dust from Brindletown was brought to the counting house during the gold rush of Burke County in 1828 where it was weighed and valued by Thomas Walton.

The gold rush in North Carolina took place in a number of counties including Burke, Guilford, Randolph, Davidson, Rowan, Montgomery, Stanly, Cabarrus, Mecklenburg, Gaston, and Union. Nash and Halifax counties in the eastern part of the state also had gold rushes. Because of the success of these gold rushes, for a time, North Carolina provided the only native gold for the United States mint. But because the state saw little profit from the gold after it was shipped to Philadelphia to be minted, North Carolina insisted upon its own government mint. The United States opened the Charlotte mint in 1837 after which time the federal government became highly involved in gold and mining enterprises in North Carolina.

Walton went on to become a prominent merchant and civic leader in Burke County. He served as the County Register (Register of Deeds) from 1752-1758, sat on the Board of Trustees for the Morganton Academy in 1818, and was a Justice of the Court of Pleas and Quarter Sessions in 1809. He was also appointed to administer Revolutionary War pensions to veterans.

Thomas Walton's home, built in 1810, was located in downtown Morganton at the northeast corner of Union and Green Streets, the location from which Walton conducted business as the Postmaster of Morganton for two terms starting in 1813. Later to be known as "Hotel Morgan," the home was located directly across the street from the home of Tod Caldwell who later became a post-Civil war governor of North Carolina.

The McEntire Inn of Morganton, built by Thomas Walton's father-in-law James McEntire, faced the courthouse on the southwest corner of South Sterling and West Union Streets. The hotel was first known as the McEntire

Inn and was operated by William ("Uncle Billy") McEntire. After the death of William McEntire, the inn became known as the Walton Hotel and was operated by Thomas Walton's grandsons, James Thomas "Jink" Walton and Edward "Stanley" Walton. Advertising for the Walton Hotel read: "Clean Beds, Comfortable Rooms, Polite and Attentive Servants, a Fine Bar, and a Free Omnibus." By 1874, the Walton Hotel, with its stagecoach office, was Morganton's largest hotel. By the late 1800s, the Walton Hotel was rented by a railroad contractor, Atwood Hunt, and it became the Hunt House. It was destroyed by fire in 1893 together with a number of other buildings in downtown Morganton.

Thomas Walton's house and store, built in 1810.

Photograph: Private collection of family.

In 1830, a private session to discuss public affairs in Burke County was held with the following persons present: Thomas Walton, Isaac Thomas Avery, Dr. R.C. Pearson, David Corpening and Francis Glass. It was determined that a contract should be drawn up for a new Burke County Courthouse before Caldwell and McDowell could officially form separate counties. By levying a tax, Burke County could be assured of sufficient funds to construct such a courthouse. In 1832, the General Assembly of North Carolina authorized the building of a two story courthouse in Morganton for $8,000, later increased to $15,000, to replace the original log courthouse built in 1785. Commissioners appointed by the General Assembly to collect funds and superintend the building of the courthouse included Thomas Walton, Captain James Murphy, John Corpening, Samuel Caldwell Tate and Colonel Isaac T. Avery. When Samuel Tate died, Dr. R.C. Pearson was chosen to take his place.

Walton and Pearson agreed that the new courthouse should be built of brick and resemble the public buildings of Charleston. Avery insisted that it be constructed of native stone, and apparently he was adamant about it. Even though the bid for a brick structure came in for $2,000 less than the plan for a stone one, the three men finally chose stone. As Walton put it, "Pearson and I tried, but Colonel Avery had stone in his head, and Pearson and I could not hammer it out."

The contractor went bankrupt during the slow, expensive process of quarrying and hauling one load of stone per day, but in the end, it all worked out: Burke County had a fine new courthouse, and Walton's daughter, Elizabeth Tilghman Walton married Avery's son, Clarke Moulton Avery.

The McEntire Inn of Morganton, built by Thomas Walton's father-in-law, James McEntire, would later become known as the Walton Hotel. Photograph by permission of *Picture Burke*, Burke County Public Library, Morganton, N.C.

♦ ♦ ♦

Thomas George Walton of North Carolina was born October 5, 1815, in Burke County. He was one of eight children born to Thomas Walton and Martha Matilda McEntire of Morganton.

Thomas George Walton married Margaret Eliza Murphy, daughter of John Hugh McDowell Murphy and Margaret Stringer Avery Murphy on December 28, 1837. John Murphy owned vast acreages and was one of the wealthiest men in western North Carolina. The two were married at "Willow Hill," the home of John Murphy's father, James Murphy, of Morganton, an Irishman who came to western North Carolina a penniless young man.

In 1845, Thomas' younger brother William McEntire Walton married his wife's younger sister, Harriet Louisa Murphy. Thomas Walton and his brother, through their marriages to the Murphy sisters, acquired large estates in money, and from their father they inherited valuable property in land and slaves. These two facts enabled them, at the time of their marriages, in 1836 and 1845, to build "Creekside" and then "Brookwood," twin plantation houses located on adjoining tracts of land in the Silver Creek Valley west of Morganton. Brookwood was destroyed by fire in 1920.

Thomas Walton and his bride lived in one large room which rested upon a stone and mortar foundation while the rest of Creekside was being built. This room would become the rear wing of Creekside.

Thomas Walton and his wife Eliza had eleven children. Of those, two died as young children: Ella Walton, in the first year of life, and Hugh Collett Walton who died at the age of nine. Hugh was killed when riding in an oxcart driven by a family slave. He fell out and the cart backed over him in the yard at Creekside. The wheels of the oxcart crushed him. Another son, John Murphy Walton, died at age 27 of tuberculosis contracted during the Civil War.

Colonel Walton was a gentleman farmer and very successful in business. After the Civil War, he managed to collect $60,000 from notes held on his father's estate. In politics, he was first an ardent Whig and later a staunch Republican after Reconstruction. My grandmother confided that her grandfather became a Republican in order to keep the taxes on Creekside low. In the post-war South, taxes were raised to approximately ten times their pre-war rate, making it difficult to retain large holdings of real property during

Reconstruction. The increased taxes were designed to force the loss of property from wealthy landowners and redistribute it to the less wealthy. This market-based system was an attempt to redress the inequities that had existed prior to the war.

Thomas George Walton was elected in 1850 to represent Burke County in the North Carolina House of Commons, now called the House of Representatives, where he signed the Western Address. The Western Address was a document which enabled western North Carolina to become more autonomous and to achieve a certain amount of political independence from more prosperous eastern North Carolina. He served one term in the North Carolina Legislature.

Thomas Walton was ardently opposed to secession, a fact outlined in his Letter of Amnesty to Governor Tod Caldwell of North Carolina. Colonel Walton was a factor in the first overturning of the secession vote in North Carolina in 1861, having cast his vote in opposition to secession. In truth, North Carolina was reluctant to secede from the Union, and did so only after war was declared and the Battle of Fort Sumter had been fought and won. In the end, reluctant North Carolinians would provide far more troops and suffer greater casualties than any other Confederate state.

Walton was named president of the Board of Directors of the Morganton Branch of the Bank of North Carolina in 1859. In 1871, he served as vice-president of the North Carolina Agricultural Society. He was appointed state agent of salt distribution for Burke County by Governor Zebulon Vance and was an active promoter for the building of the Eastern Division of the Western North Carolina Railroad. He would later serve as one

Margaret Murphy, cousin of Eliza Murphy Walton.
Photograph: Private collection of family.

of its directors in 1873. Walton was a director of the State Asylum in Raleigh (later known as Dorothea Dix Hospital) in 1897. From 1875-1877, he was one of the organizing directors and later a Secretary-Treasurer of the Western North Carolina Insane Asylum in Morganton, later called the State Hospital in 1890. This name was changed to Broughton Hospital in 1959, in honor of Governor J. Melville Broughton.

A member of Grace Episcopal Church in Morganton, Colonel Walton served as a vestryman for fifty years, and he served for many years as a lay reader in his church. In 1858, Thomas Walton became senior warden and served in that capacity until his death in 1905. Twenty-two households were listed in the church's first register; Creekside's was among them.

Colonel took a particular interest in the selection of pastors for Grace Church. When the Reverend Joseph Caldwell Huske, the first pastor ordained at Grace Episcopal, was called to serve in 1849, the Colonel held him in such high esteem he named his youngest son Herbert Huske after him.

One Christmas, the Colonel decided to provide the church with a Christmas tree. In a moment of zeal, he cut the top out of a holly tree at Creekside and donated it to the church. The old holly tree still stands on the property by the driveway, though its top has a large empty space where the branches never grew back properly.

At the beginning of the Civil War, Colonel Walton removed his two oldest sons, James and John, nicknamed "Jink" and "Jock" respectively, from military school, and together, the three of them joined the Confederate Army. Walton was commissioned Captain upon his enlistment in 1861, but resigned

Thomas George Walton, 1815-1905.
Photograph: Private collection of family.

upon reorganization of the Company in 1862. He then served as Colonel of the 8th Regiment of North Carolina Home Guards until the end of the war, encountering the forces of Kirk's Raiders in June 1864 and Stoneman's Raiders in April 1865, the former led by Union Colonel George Washington Kirk of Tennessee, also known as "Bloody Kirk," and the latter led by Union General Alvan Gillem of Tennessee.

Walton's son, James, was educated at Kings Mountain Military Academy in Yorkville, S.C. from 1855-1858 and at Hillsboro Military Academy from 1860-1861. James received a shoulder wound at Chancellorsville while serving with Company K, 33rd Regiment North Carolina Troops. He resigned from the 33rd near the end of the war to join Colonel William Holland Thomas Cavalry, the famous "Thomas Legion." Thomas Legion was unique for several reasons. Thomas was the only white man ever to serve as a Chief of the Eastern Band of Cherokees, and his soldiers were Cherokees and white men from western North Carolina and eastern Tennessee. Unlike most formations, it was a true legion, consisting of an infantry, cavalry and artillery. Thomas Legion surrendered to Union forces in Waynesville in May 1865 and theirs was officially the last shot fired in North Carolina during the Civil War.

Walton's son, John, was also educated at Kings Mountain Military Academy in 1858 and Hillsboro Military Academy from 1859 to 1861. He left school to enlist in the Civil War in July 1861 at the age of sixteen, serving under Colonel Samuel McDowell Tate and Colonel Isaac Erwin Avery, both of Morganton. His Civil War diary recounts his wartime service during 1864 and is believed to have passed down through the family of Matilda Walton Smith. John was wounded at the Battle of Appomattox which marked the end of the war and the surrender of the South.

Three historic homes in Burke County were acquired by Thomas George Walton and passed to his family. "Magnolia Place" was built in 1818 by merchant and state senator John Henry Stevelie of Switzerland. According to local legend, Stevelie lost Magnolia because of financial setbacks. In 1847, Thomas George Walton, who at that time owned Magnolia, sold it to his brother-in-law, Clarke Moulton Avery, who was married to Walton's sister Elizabeth Tilghman Walton. Magnolia Place would be enlarged by Avery to twice its size. Avery also purchased 915 acres from Walton in this transaction.

"Mountain View," located at 604 West Union Street, was originally the home of Samuel Greenlee and was built in 1815 as a rural plantation. Walton purchased Mountain View and 432 acres of land in 1872 from Emily Greenlee Happoldt for his son Stanley Walton and Stanley's wife, Kate Blackwell. Their only child, Lillian Walton, lived in the house with her husband Frederick H. Burr until his death. In 1891, Lillian Burr married Isaac Thomas Avery, Jr., and the house passed to the Avery family of Burke County.

A home known as "Fall's Castle," located at 106 Edgewood Avenue, was built by Thomas George Walton for his daughter Lucy Walton Falls in 1875 and remodeled in the early 1900s. Lucy's husband was the Reverend Neilson Falls from Baltimore who had an appointment as Rector of St. Alban's Episcopal Church in Georgetown, Washington, D.C. During that time, Reverend Falls also served as a clerk in the Surgeon General's office. Upon their return to Morganton, the couple moved into the house built for Lucy by her father. When the Falls had their furniture shipped from Georgetown to Morganton, the shipper scrawled Reverend Falls; name on the back of the headboard of his bed for identification. His antique sleigh bed remains at Creekside with his name still written on the back.

Glen Alpine Springs Hotel, built by Colonel Walton thirteen years after the war, was a popular and successful hotel located eight miles from Morganton. At that time, the hotel was the largest frame structure in North Carolina. It contained fifty rooms and was said to accommodate 100 guests. Patrons enjoyed the natural mineral springs, dancing and dining. The hotel was started in 1876 and opened for business in 1878 for a cost of $30,000. It was sold in 1900 and eventually burned down.

Colonel Walton authored, *Sketches of the Pioneers in Burke County History, North Carolina.* The book recounts anecdotal tales about members of pioneer families in Burke County. It also includes personal letters written by Colonel Walton to his wife Eliza while in camp during the Civil War and a letter written by his wife to him. The complete text of his son's (John Murphy Walton's) war time diary is included. Originally, published as a series of articles submitted to the local newspaper, the majority of articles were written in 1894 by Colonel Walton, and the last twenty pages of the book are taken from manuscripts belonging to Colonel Walton.

My grandmother told one tale about her grandfather which involved a bull he owned which he had named "Burnside" after General Ambrose Burnside, a Union general. General Burnside sported a style of bushy facial hair which became popularly known as "sideburns," and in fact these are named after him. As a commander, Burnside was instrumental in closing most of North Carolina's seaports to blockade Confederate shipments of goods and materials vital to the Confederate cause.

James "Jink" Walton and his wife Margaret
Erwin McDowell. They were devoted to one
another. When he died unexpectedly in 1916,
she lingered for a year, grief-stricken, before her
death in 1917. They were buried beside one
another at Grace Episcopal Church near their
home on South King Street. Photograph:
Private collection of family.

Burnside the bull was known for being particularly dangerous and one day lowered its head at a run to gore Colonel Walton. Fortunately, his son Herbert, who was pitching hay nearby with a pitchfork, came to his father's aid and threw the pitchfork which plunged into the bull, saving his father's life.

My grandmother, Louise Walton, recounted the following story about her grandfather's life after the Civil War:

"After the War, Colonel Walton was a great benefactor to orphaned children whose fathers had died in the conflict. Numbers of them lived for years at Creekside. Unfortunately, provisions were rather scarce and there was enough only for one large meal per day. Breakfast was very scanty, dinner at noon was as plentiful as possible, and supper was an apple which was enjoyed before a big open fire on cold days, and then it was story hour, evening prayer and bedtime."

Colonel Walton died at Creekside on June 15, 1905, at the age of 89 and is buried beside his wife in the cemetery at Grace Episcopal Church. Many of his children and grandchildren are buried nearby. Ancestors and descendants of Colonel Walton are also buried at the First Presbyterian Church in Morganton, which was founded prior to 1797, and at Forest Hill Cemetery in Morganton.

Walton's youngest child, Herbert Huske Walton, continued to live at Creekside after his marriage. He and his wife Clara Cheesborough Walton had a daughter, Louise Walton Boggs, who lived at Creekside after her marriage, raised her six children there and died in 1991.

Creekside remains in the Walton family, although most of its original 800 acres has been sold. Current residents of Creekside include myself (a great great granddaughter of Colonel Walton), my husband Kirk Emmons, and our son James Alexander ("Alex") Emmons.

The Walton Women, 1915. Granddaughters of Colonel Walton.
Photograph: Private collection of family.

Bottom Row, Left to Right:
Lila Burr Hallows, 2nd cousin
Claire Falls Barry
Eliza McKesson McNeil
Annie McKesson Leslie
Kathleen Smith Black
Tillie Falls McDowell

Top Row, Left to Right:
Janie Pearson
Augusta Falls Spurgin
Lucille Pearson
Margaret McKesson Davis
Lucy Falls Green
Kate Burr Johnson, 2nd cousin

Walton Family, c. 1890. Photograph: Private collection of family.

Front Row: Margaret Erwin McDowell Walton, wife of James Thomas Walton; James Thomas Walton; Colonel Thomas George Walton, Edward "Stanley" Walton.

Second Row: John Henry Pearson; Florence Walton Pearson, wife of John Henry Pearson; Reverend Neilson Falls; Lucy Walton Falls, wife of Reverend Neilson Falls; Kate Blackwell Walton, wife of Edward Stanley Walton; Martha Matilda Walton Smith, wife of Charles Stuart Smith; Herbert Huske Walton.

Third Row: Margaret Tilghman Walton McKesson, wife of Charles Finley McKesson; Charles Finley McKesson; Charles Stuart Smith; Lillian Walton (Burr) Avery, wife of Isaac Thomas Avery; Isaac Thomas Avery.

Child in Front Left Foreground: Neilson ("Buck") Falls. Jr.

Colonel Thomas George Walton

2. THE BUILDING OF A PLANTATION: CREEKSIDE

Creekside was built by slave labor beginning in 1836 and completed in 1837. The back wing of the house rests upon the foundation of an older pioneer era home called "Catawba Cottage," built by James Greenlee prior to the American Revolution. Thomas George Walton purchased 800 acres from James Greenlee's son, John Greenlee, including the mortar and stone foundation of Catawba Cottage which would form the foundation of the back wing of Creekside. A land grant for the original purchase of the property still exists at Creekside. Walton set about building a monumental plantation, and he had the financial and human resources to do so. He had inherited a large amount of money from his marriage to Margaret Eliza Murphy of Willow Hill, a plantation near Canoe Creek in Burke County, and he owned over 100 slaves, a considerable holding at that time.

The slave cabins were located away from the house, in an area where a railroad now runs in front of the Wal-Mart shopping center, once the location of the Henredon furniture factory. Nothing remains of the slave cabins, but somewhere in the same area are the graves of the slaves who occupied those cabins. Walton slaves are also buried in Grace Episcopal Cemetery in Burke

County. These include Abner Levi Walton (died 1869), Margaret Walton (died 1869), Patsy Walton (died 1884), and two unidentified Walton slaves, one who died in 1859 and the other in 1935. Other slaves are believed to be buried in Grace Episcopal cemetery, perhaps as many as twenty, but they lie in unmarked graves and it is not known whether any of these are Walton slaves. These slave burial sites are believed to lie one or two rows behind marked graves.

An older slave graveyard, dating back to the 1730s and owned by the Greenlee family, was situated east of Creekside and up the hill from the house. The Waltons built a large barn between the Greenlee graveyard and Creekside during pre-Civil War days. The barn would later burn down after being struck by lightning. This graveyard was located somewhere between 811 West Union Street and 819 West Union Street, but modern construction has obliterated all traces of it.

Creekside was designed by Thomas George Walton who made trips to Virginia to gather ideas for the architectural style of his home. He selected the neoclassical style known as Greek Revival which would come to represent the popular image of the antebellum plantation of the deep South. Greek Revival was a more monumental and masculine style than had been popular in the United States prior to the 1830s, and it was probably introduced to the country by Thomas Jefferson whose beloved Monticello displayed similar neoclassical features.

Thomas Walton's design was adapted from the famous drawings of Asher Benjamin, a popular architect of the 1800s who published pattern books of his designs for the public. The design of the classical mantel in the

Creekside in 1939. Photograph: Library of Congress,
Frances Benjamin Johnston.

parlor is taken directly from Benjamin's "Design for a Chimney Piece," from his book *The Architect, or Practical House Carpenter*, published in 1830.

A National Register of Historic Places Inventory by H. G. Jones (1973) for the National Park Service, Department of the Interior terms Creekside, "the most ambitious plantation house in the county (p. 3)." Thomas Tileston Watterman (1947), an influential architect and historian of the 1900s defined Creekside as "the most monumental mansion of the Piedmont" in his book *The Early Architecture of North Carolina* (p. 229).

John B. Wells (1969) of the State Department of Archives and History notes in his report to nominate Creekside for inclusion in the National Register of Historic Places:

> From the eighteenth century until Creekside was built in
> 1836, the major houses built in the Catawba Valley
> of Burke County were of Federal design. Creekside
> marks a departure from the trends then current in its
> locality and must be viewed as a house whose classic
> proportions and impressive scale make it truly outstanding (p.4).

Creekside, comprising approximately 7,000 square feet, faces Table Rock Mountain and is located near the intersection of Fleming Bypass and Highway 70 in Morganton. It contains eleven rooms including five bedrooms, four of which occupy the upper floor and a master bedroom downstairs. A living room, dining room and parlor are also located downstairs. The back wing of the house includes the kitchen, and two other rooms referred to by the family as the "Old Kitchen" and the "Old Bathroom." This original wing was once one large room which was later divided into the three rooms that currently exist in that wing. The builder, Thomas George Walton, and his bride occupied this large room while the main house was being completed.

The main house is five bricks thick with plastered interior walls, and the four massive Doric columns which support the portico are solid brick with plaster coating.

The floors of the house are made from pine which was cut on the property and heavily oiled for years until it turned black. The bricks used to build the house bear their distinctive color because of the local red clay from which they were molded.

Among the slaves who built the house were master craftsmen instructed in the carving of wood and stone decorative devices. This can be seen in the carvings located along the stringer of the staircase in the hall which contains a series of repeating wavelike patterns. Another example may be found in the fine wood carvings of oak leaves which adorn the dentils in the front of the house.

In 1886, three large iron bolts known as "hurricane bolts" were driven into the back wing of Creekside on the side which faces west. In addition, at least 10 smaller bolts were driven into the three large pilasters on the same wall. This was a response to damage caused by the great earthquake that hit Charleston, South Carolina, at 9:51 p.m. on August 31, 1886. It was the most damaging earthquake ever recorded on the eastern seaboard of the United States. Using photographic evidence and written accounts of the damage inflicted, the magnitude would later be estimated at between 7.3-7.6 on the Richter scale. People were thrown from their beds by its impact, and 90% of Charleston's historic masonry buildings were destroyed in less than sixty seconds. Legend says the earthquake generated tremendous panic among Charleston residents, and they poured out into the streets as buildings collapsed all around them.

The force of the earthquake was felt across 2 ½ million square miles—north and south from Cuba to New York, and east and west from Bermuda to the Mississippi River. Scientists estimate that aftershocks from the Charleston Earthquake were felt as long as 35 years after the quake. A large crack opened up in the wall of an upstairs bedroom at Creekside when the Charleston Earthquake hit.

The architectural features on the bottom floor of Creekside were designed to be consistently larger than those of the upper floor. The ceilings of the house reach 14 feet in height on the lower floor and 12 feet on the upper floor. The doorways on the lower floor of the main house are also taller and wider than those on the upper floor. Both upstairs and downstairs windows have 12 over 12 sash windows, but the frames, sashes and panes are larger on the lower floor.

The front hall of the house has a photograph of the builder, Thomas George Walton, in his youth. Other pictures include the first six United States presidents and the official document which identifies Creekside as a property listed on the National Register of Historic Places.

Three large antique engravings of General Robert E. Lee hang in the front hall and back hall, one with him mounted on horseback and two of him standing in uniform. A rare print of General Lee and General Stonewall Jackson mounted on horseback, titled "The Last Meeting," was taken from an original copperplate by Frederick Halperin of New York. Halperin released a limited number of these prints which were based upon an oil painting by the same name. The original oil painting of "The Last Meeting" by E.B.D. Julio

The Front Hall
Photograph: Laura Smith Shuler.

hangs in the Museum of the Confederacy in Richmond, Virginia. Though Julio never met either Lee or Jackson, he wrote to Lee in 1864 asking for his assistance in painting a monumental portrait to commemorate the final parting of Lee and Jackson on May 1, 1863 at the Battle of Chancellorsville. Lee consented, sending several photographs and a note, and Julio painted the portrait from those photographs.

Other items in the front hall include the mahogany McEntire sofa brought to the American colonies prior to the Revolution from County Tyrone, Ireland, and a grandfather clock, originally from Whitehall Plantation in Georgetown, South Carolina, which stands near the living room door. The chandelier hanging in the front hall was originally lit by gas and came from Charleston.

The house has a central hall running from front to rear with rooms on either side. Wide doorways are topped by Greek key designs and heavy chair rails. The double front doors are flanked by fanlights with diamond-shaped panes which run along the sides and over the top. Elements of the Federal style can be found in the slender stair rail with hand carved designs running along the base of the stairway.

The front hall opens into a living room and a formal parlor. The living room contains a central fireplace with an inset bookcase on one side and an inset china cabinet on the other side. The bookcase to the right of the fireplace contains books dating from the 1700s and 1800s. Practical books on tanning animal hides and guides on animal husbandry are included.

An inset china cabinet to the left of the fireplace houses a collection of Wedgwood. Across the room is a sea captain's desk, known as a secretary

The Parlor. The mantel is taken from an architectural drawing
by Asher Benjamin's popular design book, *The Architect, or Practical
House Carpenter*, 1830. Photograph: Library of Congress, Frances
Benjamin Johnston, 1939.

which came from Georgetown, South Carolina. Also in the room is the personal desk of the Reverend Mr. George Hilton, rector of Grace Episcopal Church which was a gift to Herbert Walton, and a loveseat originally owned by the McDowell family who intermarried with the Waltons.

The window sashes contain the original panes, many with small bubbles typical of hand blown glass. Until about 2008, a bottom pane in the living room bore the initials of James Willie Young Walton, Thomas George Walton's older brother, carved onto its surface with his diamond ring. The window sash fell when the original rope cords which raise and lower the window rotted, and the pane was shattered.

The parlor across the hall contains a piano bought in Philadelphia which was played by Clara Cheesborough Walton. A portrait of James Willie Young Walton by Thomas Sully hangs over the mantel. James Walton resided in Charleston, South Carolina, and was a merchant with businesses in Charleston and Alabama.

Classical plaster frescoes on either side of the fireplace are of Mercury, the messenger of the gods, and Ceres, the goddess of agriculture. These frescoes are original to the house and were given as a wedding gift to Eliza Murphy Walton. A table and a small mahogany chest in the parlor were brought over from England by the Waltons in the 1600s. Various pieces of china from the Cheesborough estate are on the piano and the mantel. Throughout the parlor are small oil landscapes by Clara Cheesborough Walton, who was an accomplished artist. A pier table featuring a mirror beneath was for ladies in long dresses to check their hemlines.

An arch divides the entry hall from the rest of the first floor, and leads to the back hall where the dining room and master bedroom are located. Each bedroom was built with its own closet, an uncommon luxury during the early 1800s when most homes used trunks or pegs for the storage of clothes. Few people owned enough clothing or material possessions to warrant the space a clothing closet would require.

The downstairs bedroom once served as the dining room, and the present dining room was once a bedroom. A small stairway used to run between the kitchen and the original dining room to facilitate the serving of meals. There is now no visible evidence to confirm the original identity of the two rooms except that where there is a closet found in each bedroom at Creekside, in this case the closet is located in the dining room rather than the bedroom. It is not clear why these rooms were switched, but my mother remembers when her grandparents still occupied the original bedroom in the 1930s.

The present day dining room contains an antique dining table purchased in Charleston. The original family banquet table was destroyed by Union troops during their occupation of the house in 1864. Only the end leaf of that banquet table remains. A mahogany sideboard from County Tyrone, Ireland, is a family piece brought over by James McEntire, the grandfather of Colonel Walton. The family china, a set of Wedgwood from England, is over 200 years old and is placed in the large breakfront china cabinet in the dining room. A mounted dinner bell hangs outside the dining room door. Dr. Charles Moncure of Virginia, married to Louisa Cheesborough of Asheville created the mounted dinner bell. The inscription, written by Byron and carved beneath the bell, reads:

The Dining Room. The piece of furniture under the window is the end piece of the original family banquet table. It bears the ink stains left by Stoneman's Raiders when General Gillem and his officers drew maps on the table. The sideboard to the right is a family piece made on the plantation. Photograph by Alex Emmons.

"That all-softening, overpow'ring knell,
The tocsin of the soul, the dinner bell."

I can remember being called to Sunday dinner by that bell in my childhood.

A small brass cup used for measuring gold dust rests on the mantel. This was the property of Thomas Walton, the father of Colonel Walton, and was used in his counting house when he worked as an assayer. Old Toby Jugs sit on a side table, purchased from a tavern in Scotland. Toby jugs were mugs designed for drinking beer and ale, and they were representations of portly old men in three-cornered hats. A small coffee grinder in the dining room belonged to Aunt Harriet, a beloved family slave.

The Blue Room in the upstairs hall contains a four poster bed which came from the Harshaw Plantation in Caldwell County. Jacob Harshaw and Alfred Dula were the largest slaveholders in western North Carolina. Other historic items on the second floor include an antique tester bed from a plantation in Summerville, South Carolina, old family photographs, ledgers from Glen Alpine Springs Hotel, accounting books from Hotel Morgan, deeds from the Murphy family, and the original land grant to the property on which Creekside was built, 800 acres located near the Catawba River, signed and sealed by Alexander Martin, Governor of North Carolina, on October 28, 1782. This document was originally owned by the Greenlee family, who sold the property to Thomas George Walton.

Historic items from the rear wing of the house include two antique spinning wheels, one of them known as a great wheel (also called a walking wheel, approximately five feet in height and used to spin wool while standing and moving the wheel with one hand. The other is a traditional

The Blue Room. The bed is from the Harshaw Plantation in Caldwell County, owned by Jacob Harshaw. Photograph by Laura Smith Shuler.

spinning wheel also called a Saxon wheel which is used for spinning flax while the operator sits at the wheel and operates a foot treadle.

A wooden box, taken by a family member from one of the battlefields of the Civil War, is part of the historic memorabilia that remains at Creekside. This kit consists of a small wooden box containing two glass bottles, four small tins and a metal ink bottle. The kit is thought to contain the personal effects of a soldier. One tin box is labeled "Sugar." The labels of the other tins are no longer readable, but they have blackened corks still in place with contents undisturbed since the Civil War. The label on one glass bottle reads: "Boykin Carmer & Company; Druggists; Baltimore, Md." The label on the other bottle reads: "C.B. Wray; Pharmacist; Yonkers, N.Y." The directions read: "Two drops. Adults. H. Nicholson."

The "dough board," one of the oldest items in the house, dates back to the 1700s. It is a somewhat irregularly shaped rectangle of marble a couple of inches thick and perhaps two feet long which sits on a table and is used for rolling out dough. The dough board has been used for making family biscuits and pie crusts for centuries.

An ornate cake pan originally owned by the Stevelie family of "Magnolia" who emigrated from Switzerland was used to make family wedding cakes. Thomas George Walton writes about this turban-shaped cake pan made of copper in his "Historic Sketches." My grandmother used this cake pan every year to make Christmas fruitcakes until tiny holes were worn in the bottom. Antique candle molds, a hanging fireplace cauldron, old iron kitchen implements, antique hot irons for pressing clothes and cobbler's tools are part of the historic items from these rooms.

The Back Hall and Stair. Photograph by Laura Smith Shuler.

A large iron plantation bell stands in the backyard at Creekside. Plantations bells were used to sound alarms, particularly in the case of fires, and also to call the slaves to the fields in the morning and home at the end of the day. They were also used for special occasions such as weddings and births.

The plantation bell at Creekside came from the Cheesborough family in Charleston and was taken to the summer home of the Cheesboroughs called

"Springvale," in Asheville, when they moved to North Carolina in 1864. Springvale fell into disrepair in the 1960s, weakened by the effects of the Flood of 1916. The family brought the bell to its final resting place at Creekside where it still stands in the back yard.

The plantation bell at Creekside.
Photograph by Alex Emmons

II. TALES FROM THE CIVIL WAR YEARS

Creekside in 1905. Photograph used by permission of *Picture Burke*, Burke County Public Library, Morganton, NC.

3. ESCAPE FROM APPOMATTOX

John Murphy Walton was born October 4, 1844 at his family home, Creekside. Nicknamed "Jock," he was the son of Colonel Thomas Walton and Eliza Murphy Walton. John attended military school at Hillsboro Military Academy in Hillsboro, North Carolina, later known as the North Carolina Military Academy. He left military training to enlist in the Civil War in 1861.

A copy of John Walton's diary, written during his wartime service, covers the period from May 17, 1864 to December 28, 1864 and is now part of the Southern Historical Collection at the Wilson Library, University of North Carolina at Chapel Hill. It recounts a portion of Walton's service as a second lieutenant in the Army of the Confederate States of America when he served in Virginia with Company B of the 6th Regiment North Carolina State Troops led by Colonel Samuel McDowell Tate of Morganton.

The 6th Regiment (also known as the "Bloody Sixth") was organized in 1861 in Alamance County, North Carolina. The regiment was composed of men from a number of counties in North Carolina including Alamance, Burke, Caswell, Catawba, Chatham, McDowell, Mecklenburg, Mitchell, Orange, Rowan, Wake and Yancey. The 6th Regiment fought in campaigns from Seven Pines to Mine Run, and in the battles of Plymouth, Cold Harbor, First and Second Manassas (also known as First and Second Bull Run), Fredericksburg, Gettysburg and Appomattox. At the time of the surrender, there were only 6 officers and 175 men remaining from an original force of approximately 2,000 men. Prominent local officers included Colonels Samuel McDowell Tate and Isaac Erwin Avery. A handsome man, Colonel Avery was killed at Cemetery Hill in the Battle of Gettysburg, in Pennsylvania, in 1863.

John Walton enlisted in the "Burke Rifles" out of Morganton as a private on July 3, 1861. He was sixteen years of age. This company became Company G of the 6th Infantry Regiment of North Carolina, and the commanding officer was Captain Clark Moulton Avery of Morganton. Walton was mustered out in November 12-13, 1861.

The "Davis Dragoons" of Morganton, Company F, in which John Walton next enlisted as a private for twelve months was composed primarily of Burke County volunteers. The Dragoons saw service from November 23, 1861 as Captain Thomas G. Walton's Company of North Carolina Volunteers. John Walton enlisted in Company F after August 1862, and on September 3, 1862, the company was assigned to the 41st Regiment N.C. Troops (3rd Regiment N.C. Cavalry).

John Walton then joined Company B, 6th Regiment in Orange County, on March 22, 1864, as a second lieutenant and was accounted for by muster rolls through February 1865. It was during this time that his Civil War diary was penned.

Walton's diary recounts a number of interesting moments in history, much of it under fire. He relates skirmishing with the enemy, the building of breastworks, taking part in the destruction of railroads in Virginia, and enduring the dry dusty summer and periods of heavy rains. On a more personal note, he relates bouts with dysentery, a common malady of the Civil War soldier, and he tells on one occasion of riding in the ambulance, an army wagon, because he is too ill to march. He recounts marching through the Shenandoah Valley of Virginia and how the mountains remind him of his home in western North Carolina. He finds the community in the Valley hospitable and kind, and writes of being fed milk, butter, apple butter and light bread, probably an uncommon treat at that harsh time in the war.

Walton's company marches into Lexington and through the graveyard with arms reversed, a position in which guns are held upside-down and backwards, with the muzzle facing behind and down toward the ground. This position was ordered out of respect for the fallen soldiers of the Confederacy. While in Lexington, the company stops to observe General Stonewall Jackson's grave. General Jackson, a hero of the Confederacy, had fallen in the Battle of Chancellorsville the year prior, much to the grief of the South which had depended upon his extraordinary gifts as a military strategist. The numbers who attended Jackson's funeral were staggering; only George Washington's funeral had more mourners, and even Abraham Lincoln's funeral did not draw the numbers that Jackson's did.

Walton recounts having been shelled by the enemy from the heights of Harper's Ferry in West Virginia. He also tells of crossing the Potomac River as the Confederate Army moves toward Washington, D.C. A family footnote in the diary reveals that Walton later told his sister Florence Walton Pearson that the men crossed the Potomac three abreast with a short man between two taller ones. John Walton himself was a short man as was his father,

Colonel Walton.

His diary recounts approaching Washington, D.C. and coming within five miles of the city on July 11-12, 1864 before being repulsed. General Jubal Early led the march that the Union feared might overrun Washington, D.C., but hopes of his victory were thwarted by Union General Lew Wallace.

On Monday, July 18, 1864, Walton relates he has heard that Union troops have made a raid on Morganton. He expresses his anxiousness to have details of this raid on his home town. The skirmish he speaks of was probably the raid on Camp Vance on June 13, 1864, led by General George W. Kirk ("Bloody Kirk") and his band of bushwhackers known as "Kirk's Raiders." Camp Vance, less than six miles from Morganton, was a training camp for Confederate soldiers conscripted into the army. The camp was captured by Kirk in the raid. Walton's father, Colonel T.G. Walton, commander of the 8th Home Guard, with a force of up to 300 Confederates, skirmished with Kirk during that raid, but the Home Guard was strung out for a mile along a mountain road with no space to form and was forced to fall back.

John Walton recounts the events of July 28, 1864 when an election for Governor of North Carolina is held in camp with Zebulon Baird Vance winning unanimously. Colonel Tate makes a speech, the men cheer and the band plays "Dixie."

Walton recounts the distressing news received on September 7, 1864 that General Sherman has taken Atlanta in the Battle of Atlanta. This event, which marked the start of Sherman's "scorched earth" campaign of destruction in his March to the Sea, took place on September 3, 1864.

Moments of quiet and simple times are also reflected in John Walton's diary. Always tidy by nature, he speaks on numerous occasions of taking baths with friends and commanding officers. He relates that he and his fellow soldiers forage for corn and apples and that his commanding officers hunt for turkey to serve at Thanksgiving. His thoughts are often about home, and he recounts when he has written to and received letters from family members. He records on one occasion that he has had a coat and vest cut out to be made for him and on another occasion when camp life is monotonous, he makes a chimney for his quarters.

Wounded at the Battle of Appomattox, John Walton lay in the hospital at the time of General Lee's surrender. Neither he nor his surgeon wished to surrender to the Union, so Walton crawled from his bed, and together they made their escape. Family legend says they ate blackberries to stay alive on the journey home. At one point, the two stopped for the night at a house on the Dan River in Pittsylvania County, Virginia. The occupants of the house took the men in and fed them. At the table, the lady of the house overheard her guest being called "Walton," and replied, "That is my maiden name. Where are your ancestors from?" When Walton told her his people were originally from neighboring Amherst County, Virginia, she replied, "Why, you are my cousin!" The next morning when John Walton and his surgeon were to resume their journey south, the lady insisted he take a horse the family owned rather than the mule he was riding. He rode the poor animal until it dropped dead, whereupon he continued his journey on foot.

John Walton returned to Creekside after the surrender, arriving at daybreak one morning. He sent a slave in to wake his mother who went out to greet him, and he requested that water and clean clothing be brought to him so his sisters would not see him in his unkempt state. After bathing and dressing, he burned his ragged clothes and went into the house to see his family.

John Walton's recovery from the rigors of war was never fully realized; he had contracted tuberculosis during his wartime service and died seven years after the war on December 2, 1872 at the age of twenty-seven. Legend says that he stumbled on the stair as he made his way to the upstairs bedrooms after his long walk home from Virginia. Members of the family for generations have told of hearing the sound of footsteps climbing the stairs in the quiet of the night and heard the stumble on the steps.

◆ ◆ ◆

On a less somber note, I will relate two humorous experiences I had in the 1990s while visiting the site of another famous battlefield, that of Gettysburg. I spent several days with my family walking the quiet green fields of that horrific battle, the largest battle ever waged in the Western Hemisphere. We read the monument inscriptions, traced the troop movements of Union and Confederate forces, and stood on the line where the troops of Pickett's Charge bravely stepped forward in a mile long walk to certain death. We picked our way carefully among the rocky outcroppings of Devil's Den, and stood on Little Round Top where General Chamberlain charged the troops of Alabama in a startlingly decisive move for an inexperienced commander.

At the end of an exhausting and rather melancholy day, we returned to the Civil War Museum. I went to the counter of the gift shop to purchase a small item. Making small talk, the clerk asked if I was from the area. "Oh no, I'm from the South," I replied. He laughed and said, "Oh, well then, I have a joke for you! It goes like this:

"During the War, a group of Confederates came upon a despondent soldier standing on a wooden bridge, staring silently down into the swirling waters. Fearful that he was contemplating suicide, the soldiers quickly rallied around him to encourage him. 'Think about your dear mother and father!' they cried. 'My mother and father are dead,' came the quiet reply. 'Think about your beloved wife and children,' they suggested. 'I'm not married,' he said. 'Well, then, think about General Lee!' they shouted in unison. 'Who?' he queried. 'Jump, Yankee, jump!' they cried.

The other amusing incident took place one evening in the historic downtown area of Gettysburg. My family and I took part in a candlelight ghost tour known as the Farnsworth House Ghost Walks and Mourning Theater hosted by a man in period costume carrying a lantern. We arrived at the designated location and walked about the town as a group, stopping at homes and businesses purported to be haunted by the restless spirits of another century. After we completed the tour, we stopped for a drink and something to eat at a downtown eatery in the historic district. When we left, we took a shortcut across the grass and headed for our car in the dark.

Clearly, another walking ghost tour was in progress, for we saw the lantern held by the host, and we saw a huddle of ghost hunters gathered around him. "Shhh," I said to my family, "we need to be quiet. A ghost tour is going on over there." So we silently moved across the grass through the darkness so as not to disturb anyone. "Look over there!" someone hissed, and we heard a collective gasp. Camera flashes went off as the group took multiple shots of my family. We couldn't help but laugh out loud. Almost at the same instant, everyone in my party made ghostly wailing sounds between choking laughter and ran on across the grass to the parking lot.

4. THE UNION OCCUPATION

Contrary to popular local myth, Yankee troops did not ride their horses through the wide front doors and down the halls of Creekside during their occupation of the house and grounds. These legends state that the marks of horses' hooves remain on the front hall floors. Such tales are not true, though they are colorful and in keeping with the fascinating incidents that actually did occur during the Union occupation.

Union General William Sherman's mission in the Civil War was threefold: to defeat Southern armies in the field, to destroy the Confederacy's material resources, and to erode the South's will to wage war. In order to achieve this end, Sherman relentlessly struck at both the military might of the South and its civilian population. His goals were to capture Atlanta, which provided the industrial might of the South, to punish the state of South Carolina for its role in initiating secession from the Union, and to deprive both the military and civilian populations of food, shelter and security. His passionately vengeful strategy instigated a path of death and destruction previously unseen in the war.

The Carolina's Campaign was born of Sherman's determination to finish what his March to the Sea had begun. After capturing Savannah, his plan was to turn north and sweep through the Carolinas, targeting South Carolina in particular. When ordered by his commander, General Ulysses S. Grant to reinforce the Army of the Potomac in the floundering Siege of Petersburg, Sherman instead persuaded Grant that he would be far more useful in destroying everything of value to the southern military in his northward march.

Sherman's strategy was to scatter his forces in multiple directions in order to confuse his enemy. Many thought General Sherman's hidden goal was to destroy Charleston, when it fact it was his plan to burn Columbia, the capital of South Carolina. Sherman succeeded in his plan, destroying by fire in February 1865 one of the most beautiful and classically designed cities of the old South. Though Sherman denied he had ordered the firing of Columbia, he stated that he had never shed a tear when it happened. His Carolina's Campaign would culminate with the Battle of Bentonville in North Carolina in March 1865 with the defeat of Confederate General Joseph E. Johnston.

The 2nd Army of the Ohio, designated the Center Wing of Sherman's army, was ordered to fight in the final phase of the Carolina's Campaign. Between March and May of 1865, General George Stoneman of the 2nd Army of the Ohio, and 6,000 cavalrymen, known as Stoneman's Raiders, moved from Tennessee through western North Carolina and Virginia destroying bridges and railroads, disrupting commerce, and raiding the storehouses which provided food and supplies to the failing Confederacy. The intention of Stoneman's campaign was not to engage in battle but to destroy public works and to block the supply lines to Lee and his Army of Northern Virginia. Thousands of prisoners were taken by Stoneman's army, and tremendous damage was inflicted in western North Carolina during this

Major General George Stoneman, 2nd Army of the
Ohio. Photograph: Library of Congress.

Major General Alvan Gillem, 10th Regiment Tennessee
Infantry (Union). Photograph: Library of Congress.

period. Stoneman's Raiders moved from town to town, burning public buildings, looting private homes, and harassing private citizens. Stoneman intended to free Union prisoners held in Salisbury Confederate Prison, the only Civil War prison camp in North Carolina, but when his army arrived in Salisbury in April 1865, they found the prisoners had been moved two months prior. Stoneman set fire to the prison.

General Alvan C. Gillem, under Stoneman's command, led a brigade of cavalry through Morganton and Lenoir in mid-April 1865. General Gillem, born in Jackson County, Tennessee, and educated at the United States Military Academy, seemed particularly determined to prove that his allegiance did not lie with his southern brothers. Tales spread about the ferocity and ruthlessness of Gillem and his men, who were said to bear little respect for their commander and far less for the rebels they encountered which included largely women, children, old men, and disabled former soldiers of the Confederacy.

During this time, Colonel Walton commanded the 8th Regiment of North Carolina Home Guards and engaged Union troops in a fight near the Catawba River at a place known as Rocky Ford. Walton had directed that earthworks be erected on the south side of the Catawba River where a low bridge provided a crossing point for Union troops. Having been provided a cannon by Governor Vance, the Home Guard kept up continuous fire on a large contingent of Union troops until they were forced to cross the Catawba at another point farther down the river called Flemming's Ford. When their cannon was destroyed by enemy artillery, the Home Guard was forced to withdraw.

At the Old Burke County Courthouse, the earliest public records of the town were burned and many homes in downtown Morganton were ransacked by General Gillem's men. The Raiders were joined by freed slaves and Union sympathizers from the area. Fortunately, the citizens of Morganton had been warned of the approach of General Gillem's cavalry, and had time to stash their valuables in hidden places. The raiders, however, employed great ingenuity in discovering most of these hidden valuables.

The following tale is taken from an account written by my grandmother whose byline reads "As told to Louise Walton by 'Aunt' Harriet (a former slave):"

"At Creekside, Aunt Harriet wrapped up the family silver and placed it in the root cellar, known to the family as the 'potato hole.' It remained undiscovered by Union troops. Later that night, she slipped the big sack of silver out of the potato hole and crept past the Yankees who were making merry around a big campfire in the yard. Once she stepped on a twig and one blue clad soldier stood up listening, but she remained unseen. Aunt Harriet slipped away and buried all the silver on the big hill in front of the house, but she placed it under several different trees so if one lot was discovered, there would still be silver left. There it remained until after the War. One lot of the silver is still in use at Creekside, another lot could not be located by Aunt Harriet as trees were cut during the war years for firewood. The third lot of silver was stolen from her and little Miss Tillie Walton as they returned from the woods with it in 1865, after the war. A Yankee carpetbagger snatched it out of Miss Tillie's hand as she was taking it home in her sunbonnet. Aunt Harriet struck him with her old wooden walking stick, but he just laughed and stuffed the silver in the big bag he carried over his shoulder. He threw Miss

Tillie's sunbonnet in a mud puddle."

Creekside's occupation by Union troops took place during this time period. General Gillem and a brigade of Union cavalry rode up the front walk of Creekside, and Colonel Walton met them on the steps of his home. Colonel Walton greeted General Gillem with the words: "On your honor as a gentleman, I entrust my home and family to your care, sir." It is possible that Colonel Walton's deference to General Gillem saved his home from destruction, though furniture and provisions were destroyed and Gillem and his men headquartered there.

General Gillem and his officers slept in the bedrooms at Creekside during their occupation. Other members of Gillem's cavalry slept on the back porch of the house. A former house slave named 'Uncle' Alfred, a loyal servant who remained behind after Lincoln's emancipation of the slaves, spent each night during the occupation stretched out on a pallet in front of his mistress' bedroom door to protect her from invading troops and, indeed, she never came to any harm thanks to Alfred's vigilance and bravery.

The soldiers who stayed on the long back porch slept on small forged iron camp beds they brought with them. The foot and head of these camp beds consisted of two narrow iron posts each with curved feet for a base, connected by a horizontal iron crosspiece at the top. Two or three planks were laid across these foot high iron supports to fashion a kind of "sawhorse" bed. Two bolts on each support were used to tighten the planks together to keep them from shifting. The planks needed to complete these camp beds were carried on wagons behind the troops. Though hard and uncomfortable and with only minimal width, scarcely enough to allow one to turn over at night, these camp beds nevertheless kept the occupant off the cold, damp ground. When the army broke camp and moved on, these beds were loaded back into the wagon until the next bivouac.

An artifact of the Union occupation at Creekside is one of these forged camp bed frames left behind by the Union army, known by the family as the "Yankee bench." Though covered with rust, the supports to this bed still exist and, until recently, have served as a garden bench. All that was required were three narrow wooden planks laid across the frame to create a nice iron bench. Though a bit low to the ground, I sat on this bench during my childhood. It is now stored indoors where the weather will not further deteriorate it.

During the Union occupation, it was necessary for the General and his officers to plan a strategy for continued movement through North Carolina. General Gillem and members of his staff sat around the dining room table at Creekside, known as the banquet table, to devise their troop movements. Maps laid on the table during these strategy sessions leaked ink onto its surface, and these stains remain to this day as testament to the presence of the enemy. The only existing section of the banquet table is one of the end leaves with a silver label identifying it as having been made in Baltimore, Maryland. Yankee soldiers dragged the table out into the yard to write letters on, eat on, and to finally chop up and burn for firewood. The remaining leaf of the banquet table, which is kept in the dining room and now used as a side table, still bears the ink stains from that historic encounter.

Upon their departure from Creekside, General Gillam's men opened the jars of canned goods stored in the pantry and ran their hands through them, rendering the food unfit for human consumption. The remaining members of the household were women, children and old men now left without provisions. My great great grandmother, Eliza Murphy Walton, and the house servants, emptied out the jars and reboiled the contents to save what they could. These canned goods, together with whatever could be foraged, comprised the daily fare of the family. Gillem's men took the few farm animals which were left to feed their army. Such tales of misery and hunger were common across the South toward the end of the war.

One interesting artifact of the Union occupation is the existence of a profuse quantity of wild onions in the yard around Creekside. My grandmother, and family members before her, always swore the horses of Union cavalrymen carried the wild onions in their hooves and spread them around the yard as they moved about. In fact, wild onions can be spread by seed, so this tale as odd as it may sound is likely true.

5. "AUNT" HARRIET

Every Civil War plantation had a caretaker for the children of the family, one who taught them their manners, guided them and watched over them. Known as the "mammy," this position was at the pinnacle of the hierarchy of the slave system. Because the mammy guarded and befriended the future generations of the plantation, she was held in great esteem and afforded more benefits than her fellow slaves and usually regarded as a house servant more than anything else.

At Creekside, the mammy was "Aunt" Harriet. She was beloved by the family and earned the great respect of all who knew her. My grandmother, Louise Walton Boggs, was raised by Aunt Harriet who remained with the family after the Civil War until her death. At this point, I turn the narrative over to my now deceased grandmother, Louise Walton Boggs, who penned her own family tales which were never published but which still exist as "Tales of Creekside: Historical and Supernatural:"

"Aunt Harriet was, first of all, the much-loved tiny Negro maid who sat at my great grandmother, Martha Walton's feet. She always talked lovingly of 'Old Miss.' Old Miss spoiled her and gave her licorice sticks to chew and sometimes a little drink Aunt Harriet called "pernady." This was water, sugar, spice and a little wine. Once some distinguished guests were calling at the old brick home which has long stood in Morganton, and time came for Aunt Harriet's favorite drink. "Miss," she said, "I wants my pernady." Her mistress ignored her. A few minutes later she called out louder, "Miss, I said I *wants* my pernady." So her mistress excused herself from her guests and went for the drink."

Regarding Aunt Harriet's appreciation for "pernady," I have often wondered if the drink my grandmother was referring to might actually be the liqueur called Pernod, which my research indicates is often mixed with sugar and water. Pernod was first distilled by a French physician in 1792 as a medicinal remedy for his patients. The original liqueur contained wormwood, a hallucinogen, which was banned from the drink in 1915. The modern Pernod, without the inclusion of its dangerous ingredient, nevertheless retains its distinctive licorice flavor derived from anise and other botanicals.

My grandmother's narrative continues: "After his mother's death, my grandfather brought Aunt Harriet to Creekside. She nursed and cared for every child and grandchild in the family. I was her last charge. She was very old, but ruled me with a kind, firm hand. She smoked a corncob pipe and wore a white apron, but liked her head-handkerchiefs either red or blue. Her face was like dark, hard leather, but felt firm when I kissed it. She often said, 'I'm looking for Judgment Day, when old 'Massa' and the good Lord is coming in that fiery chariot to take me to Heaven.'"

Aunt Harriet had her own room at Creekside, known to the family as "Aunt Harriet's Cellar," for it was located in the back wing of the house and was actually the dirt-floored cellar. This room remains much as it was prior to the Civil War. The earthen floor is hard-packed and the ceilings are somewhat low though one can stand up in the cellar with no problem as long as one stoops to enter the door. Measuring approximately 17 feet x 20 feet, Aunt Harriet's cellar room was probably the size of a one room cabin of its day. A fireplace made of large stones and with a sizable hearth extending outward with a stone ledge is situated along one wall of the room, and bare rafters comprise the ceiling. The room has changed little since Aunt Harriet occupied it, though no original furnishings remain. One would imagine that the furnishings for a house servant of that time would have been few, probably a bed, a chair and table, and a few cooking utensils.

I remember my grandmother telling the story of how Aunt Harriet made "hoecakes," which were a common food item during the Civil War, probably similar to cornbread. She mixed up the dough and patted it onto the blade of a hoe which was then set near the fire to bake. Hoecake was a southern staple comprised of cornmeal, salt, and water, and sometimes sweetened with sugar, not unlike modern cornbread, but cooked in whatever utensil was at hand—a frying pan, a hoe blade, and sometimes simply placed in the ashes of a fire.

Aunt Harriet, born a slave, raised several generations of Walton children and died at Creekside at the age of ninety. She took great pride in her ancestry, often saying, "I'se pure African." A fascinating turn of the century picture included in this book shows Aunt Harriet in her last years, long after emancipation, holding a book in her hands as if reading to a young girl who is my grandmother Louise Cheesborough Walton. In fact, Aunt Harriet, like most slaves, was unable to read and the book was held in her hands as a prop.

An interesting footnote to this tale is my grandmother's recollection of the death of Aunt Harriet. My grandmother's room was on the upper floor of

Creekside and located above the cellar where Aunt Harriet lived, two floors below. On the night Aunt Harriet died, my grandmother rested uneasily in her bed. In the dark, early hours of the morning, she was started to observe a white mist rising slowly up through the floor of her bedroom in a spiral until it disappeared through the ceiling. The next morning when she learned that Aunt Harriet had died during the night, she remembered the strange white mist and always believed it was the soul of Aunt Harriet rising to meet God.

Aunt Harriet with my grandmother, Louise Cheesborough
Walton, circa 1907. Photograph: Private collection of family.

Clara Cheesborough Walton.
Photograph: Private collection of family.

6. CIVIL WAR LETTERS AND DOCUMENTS

A number of letters exchanged between family members at Creekside during the Civil War still exist. Photocopies of these letters have been included in this book, together with transcriptions. Among these are four letters from Colonel Walton to his wife Eliza Murphy Walton while at Wilmington, Camp Anderson, Camp Heddrick and Camp Wyatt in North Carolina, written between January and April of 1862. All of Colonel Walton's letters to his wife were embossed with a tiny rose in the upper left hand corner. A letter written by Colonel Walton to his cousin Jessie Webb five years before Walton's death is included.

Hundreds of Civil War documents including bills of sale, deeds, ledger entries and promissory notes remain at Creekside. Photocopies and transcriptions of twelve important documents and related letters are also included, some of them owned by the family and others gathered from the Rebel Archives of the Record Division of the War Department.

These papers include two documents from the Office of the Provost Marshall General of the Army of the Ohio, one permitting Colonel Walton to pass through the lines to return to his home after the surrender, and the other an oath of allegiance taken by Colonel Walton, a stock certificate from the Western North Carolina Rail Road Company; a transcription of the medical diploma of Dr. John Alfred Walton, Colonel Walton's brother; the Amnesty Papers of Colonel Walton, including a letter of recommendation from Governor Tod Caldwell and an accompanying document on which Thomas Walton swears to uphold the Constitution and the laws regarding the emancipation of slaves; four letters recommending that John M. Walton be made a Cadet; and a letter of welcome to Clara Cheesborough upon her engagement to Herbert Walton.

The following is a letter from Colonel Thomas Walton to his wife while in camp in Wilmington:

Wilmington, Jan 16th, 1862

"My beloved Wife,

I have no doubt you have been disappointed at not hearing from me before this but I have had no opportunity of writing until now. We reached here safely on to day being six days on the march from Goldsboro' we staid six days at G. by direction of Genl. Gatlin to refresh the men and horses, Jink [his son James Thomas Walton] and Stuart arrived the day before we left. I went immediately to the post office on my arrival here and found as I expected a letter from my dear Wife. I am relieved to hear that you bear our separation so much better than I feared. Your letter read at Goldsboro (by Jink) containing the love pledges of my dear children almost unmanned me for the time, kiss them over and over again for me and tell them how much Father prized their little missives of affection, and that I shall be disappointed if Mothers next letter does not contain something from them. I stayed last night with Mr. Hasell Burgevina (?) and sister. He lives 8 miles from

Wilmington in a (?) of opulence and polish living in an ancient dwelling built in the Old English style by his Grandfather an Englishmen, the house is in a fine state of preservation and kept precisely as it was left by his ancestor, they are church people and great admirers of the Bishop. Lieut. Tate [Samuel McDowell Tate] and Avery [Isaac Erwin Avery], Jink and myself took supper with them, Tate and myself staid all night and enjoyed the luxury of a good bed, the sister Miss Sallie is a maiden of some thirty five years, not handsome but very intelligent and agreeable, she insisted on my coming to see them as often as an opportunity occurred, and Mr. Burgevina made me promise if Jink should get sick during our stay near Wilmington that I would send him to his house to be nursed by his wife and sister, his wife was not at home being on a visit to her relatives in Virginia. I paid my respects to Genl. Anderson today and am favorably impressed with him, he said he would do all in his power to give my troops as healthy a locality for our quarters as the vicinity afforded, and sent Major Lamb the Quarter Master with me to examine two localities and I am going tomorrow to look at another. I think we will be situated about 3 miles from town and perform such duties as the General may assign us, there is a good deal of sickness amongst the troops here principally measles and mumps, one of my men (Fitzgerald) broke out with measles to day. I sent him to the hospital by direction of the Genl. the balance are all well with good appetites. Flour is very high here worth $12 per barrel and difficult to get. Our baggage has all reached here safely. Stuart and Jink left it between Salisbury and Raleigh the conductor refusing to bring it on. I detailed Mr. Moore from Goldsboro, and he finally succeeded in getting it on. I have not had time to examine its condition but hope to find it all right. We are tonight in a large comfortable house in the suburbs, and I am now writing by a comfortable fire. Yesterday was the most unpleasant experience since we left home, the transitions from warm to cold in this region are sudden and extreme and this fact must make it in some degree unhealthy, the better class look ruddy and healthy while the lower look sallow and squalid, the greater portion of Duplin and New Hanover Counties passed over by us is miserably arid and unproductive, covered with the everlasting long leaf pine, varied by cypress swamps, the boughs of the cypress festooned with the long moss which seems to be the gloomy offspring of the miasmatic pools in which they flourish. The Bishop is here I have not seen him as yet but hope to do so tomorrow. In regard to Jocks going to school I hope you will send him where you think best I know he ought to be somewhere and hope you will impress the importance of his acquiring a good education upon him. I am sorry to hear Wm. failed in getting Claywell to take the house, tell him he had better employ Leigh or Shell to reroof it while it is idle, and to have the Ice house fixed up and filled if an opportunity offers. I expect you and Mr. Stacy [probably the overseer] will manage the farm matter, as well or better than it would be done if I was at home. I don't know when I shall get to see you dear Wife unless you come to see me. It would if anything could add to the pleasure to see my dear children but this I know cannot be now. There has been a great deal of excitement here growing out of a message rec'd from Senator Geo Davis of the place stating that Genl. Beauregard had telegraphed to Richmond that Burnside's fleet was (?) for this place, as he has failed so far to make his appearance the excitement has in some measure subsided. I do not see that the prospect for peace is more flattering than when I left, unless the financial difficulties in which the Northern (?) say the Lincoln government is involved, may have the effect. Reeves does remarkably well better than I expected, he and Lieut. Tate's boy cook for our mess, and I assure you do very well. Reeves makes better corn bread than we have at home, so far as wheat bread is concerned we have (?) chewed it, we have had fritters occasionally. I do not think we will need a stove until we get a house to go in. You may assure yourself that I will not subject myself to unnecessary exposure. Your letter was dated the 9th and I read it on the 18th. I will look for another from either you Mag or Hal today. I gave I.W. McElrath money to buy a barrel of yams for you. I hope he does so. I don't believe I have indulged in so many endearing expressions sweet wife this time, and if you don't like it you must blame yourself, as all the letters I have read from you caution me that others open and read mine. I don't see why you would object to Stan [his son Stanley Walton] doing so for I suppose he has no objection to his Father telling his Mother that he loves her as (he does) above all earthly things.

Truly yrs, TGW"

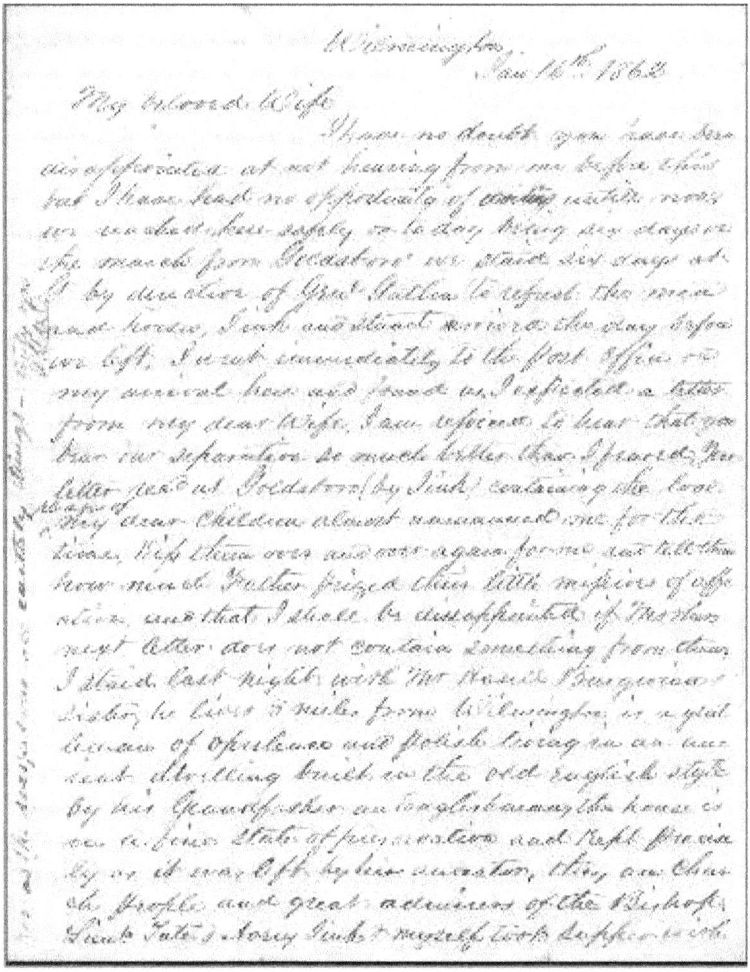

Wilmington
Jan 16th 1863

My beloved Wife

I have no doubt you have been disappointed at not hearing from me before this but I have had no opportunity of writing until now we reached here safely to day being six days on the march from Goldsboro' we staid six days at it by direction of Genl [illegible] to refresh the men and horses, Tink and [illegible] arrived the day before we left. I went immediately to the Post Office on my arrival here and found as I expected a letter from my dear Wife, I am rejoiced to hear that you bear our separation so much better than I feared. Your letter recd at Goldsboro (by Tink) containing the love messages of my dear Children almost unmanned me for the time, kiss them over and over again for me and tell them how much Father prized their little missives of affection, and that I shall be disappointed if Mother's next letter does not contain something from them. I staid last night with Mr [illegible] [illegible] [illegible] he lives 3 miles from Wilmington, is a gentleman of opulence and polish living in an ancient dwelling built in the old English style by his Grandfather an Englishman the house is in a fine state of preservation and kept precisely as it was left by his ancestor, they are Church people and great admirers of the Bishop. Lieut [illegible], [illegible] Tink & myself took supper with

Camp Anderson 3 miles East of Wilmington Jan'y 23d 1862

"My dear Wife,

I have been much disappointed in not hearing from home this week, yours of the 9th (?) being the last I have rec'd and which I answered immediately. I hope to get one to day. We are encamped as you see by the heading within 3 miles of W. [Wilmington]. Genl. A. [Anderson] was kind enough to give me choice of three localities and after a thorough examination I have determined on this as being the most healthful and convenient, it is situated near the residence of an Old English Gardener who with his wife comprise the whole of his white family, they are very kind and he readily gave up for the Officers' Quarters a house which we find convenient and will be comfortable so soon as we get a stove, his name is Hopkins and from appearances seems to be skillful and tasteful as a Florist and Horticulturist, the old lady says they have a great many beautiful flowers in their season and the grounds are filled with rare evergreens. I am writing in his parlor by a good fire which I assure you is very comfortable today. The weather here seems to be very variable on Tuesday being so warm that most of the men threw off their coats being oppressed with the heat, but today (Thursday) and yesterday a strong North Easter has been blowing accompanied with rain of an icy coldness. I have been very busy superintending the erection of our stables which I think we can finish the 1st fair day. The men are still in tents but lumber will be supplied us, and we purpose beginning our shanties as soon as the shelter for our horses are completed. I have seen very little of Wilmington as yet, and found no acquaintances except among the Officials of the Army. The Bishop called to see me before we left town and invited me to call on him which I have not done as yet. I went to the church he preaches in twice on Sunday he did not preach in the morning but did at night, delivering his usual clear masterly style a most admirable sermon on the present crisis. I wish my dearest Eliza you could have been present, abounding as it did in consolations to those who have dear friends and relatives in the service of their country. The Bishop said he has not the slightest doubt the whole was directed by the providence of God and that the calamity and sufferings we are undergoing will be beneficial in their final results. That the returning of the people as a whole in the Southern Confederacy to the Lord their God repenting of their former sins would bring the war to a close sooner than if the navies of all Europe were to join our standard. We have not as yet heard of the destruction of Burnside's fleet. Genl. Anderson was under some apprehension that it might be intended for W. [Wilmington] and as we are encamped only 5 miles from the coast advised me to be very vigilant for fear of a surprise, tho' other officers seem to think there is not the slightest danger, I do not suppose we will be called on to perform very arduous duties until our quarters are erected, and we are instructed in some degree in the drill, a Capt. Haxall (?) was recommended for that purpose and I have accepted him, he is from Virginia and is one of the Genls aides. Tell Stanley I met with his friend Mr. Cotter who seemed delighted at seeing me, he stayed with us until 9 o'clock at night I told him that Stanley and Wm were coming to see us after a while and he seemed to be as much pleased as though he was going to meet a relation from whom he had been long separated, he belongs to a Cavalry Company gotten up very much in the same way ours was. I also met with Mark Erwin & Andy Shuford (Dr. Sudderth's father in law) I learned from Shuford that Mark has been very steady ever since he joined Green's (?) Battalion, they are located about 4 miles from us at Mitchells Sound. My Lieuts are behaving very well now and I think Willoughby will and has improved in his habits, W.B. Avery has measles and I think will do well he has taken a room with the Gardener and has very comfortable quarters, he seems to be low spirited today, which I suppose arises from the fact that (?) began in the same way. I see no reason for apprehending sickness here there is certainly no local cause for it very near us. Mr. Hopkins says it is the healthiest place in the world as he is satisfied from a twenty year residence without sickness. I begin to want to see my dear wife and children very much, but cannot at present make any calculation when I can do so now; do write every week as it is a great comfort to get your letters. Tell Hugh he must not forget (?) & Billy Bethel. Tell him everybody says Billy is the best horse in the Company. Tell George I had to let Jink have Ball to ride for the present, his horse being so much reduced by distemper as to be unfit for service for some time. I don't think I ever saw a horse suffer so much; he had to be lanced in four places and ran gallons. George Moore is a smart boy and very useful to his father they have gone to day to see the ocean, and I think will pay dearly for the sight as it still rains and is bitter cold. Tell Florence Father misses her good night kiss of affection, and I want her to kiss Mother for me every night as well as for herself. Tillie [daughter Martha Matilda Walton] must learn more pretty songs to sing for me when I (?) Lucy [daughter Lucy Walton] must keep dear Mother's spirits up by her frolicsome mimicry. Tell Mag [daughter Margaret Tilghman Walton] I won't send her a kiss until she writes to me, dear little Herbert [son Herbert Huske Walton] is walking. How I should like to ride him on my knee this evening. I send a messenger every day with my morning report to headquarters and get my papers and letters I will not close this until he returns with a letter from you I hope—"

[The letter continues with a message beginning "Dear Mother" may have been written by John Murphy Walton who served with his father Colonel Walton.]

"Dear Mother,

Pa has left room enough for me to write a few lines. I suppose he has written to you about our safe arrival all except the boxes which came on safe afterwards. I do not think that Jink's has come, he heard it was in Goldsboro. I suppose he will get it in a few days. I am very sorry that you did not put in my uncle's shirt as I am very much in need of it. Pa told me yesterday that he could spare me one. If I get it I can do with (?) more. I was looking through my valise yesterday and found you had not put up all my collars. If Stanley comes down you can send them by him. I was thinking as we came down from Goldsboro how you would like to have some of the fine sweet..."

(next sheet)

[This letter continues onto another sheet which has become separated from the main letter over time.]

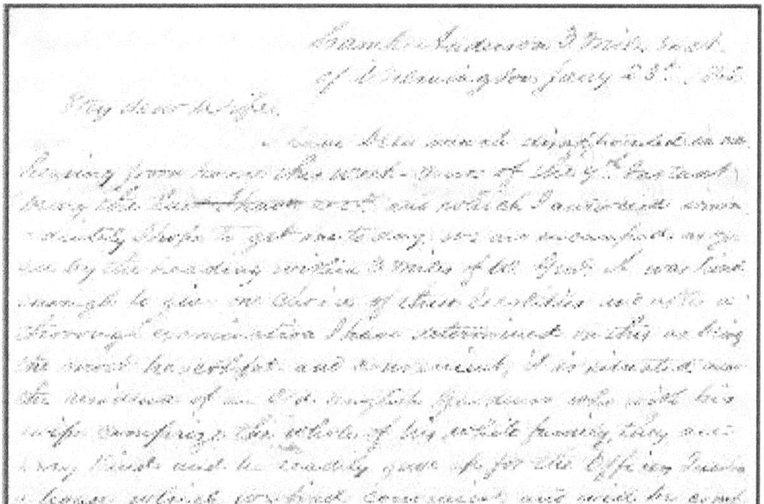

Camp Heddrick April 2d '62

"My dear Wife,

I received your welcome letter last night and enjoyed it very much. I hope the next will come sooner and be longer; you will see from the station this is dated from, that we have left our old quarters. We left on last Sunday afternoon at ½ past 4 o'clock p.m. and reached here at 10 o'clock p.m., a distance of 20 miles, over a heavy sand road. I felt very reluctant to leave our old quarters after having done so much work in order to make ourselves comfortable, but am very well satisfied with that change, so far as I am personally concerned; the officers have very nice comfortable quarters, and more satisfactory than all, I have a room to myself which can be kept clean and private when I desire it. This camp is situated on the Cape Fear about 1 ½ miles from Fort Fisher and 1 mile from the ocean. I have not been to the Fort but understand it is very strong, having (?) heavy casemated or bomb proof guns and 24 not casemated there are about 1,800 or 2,000 troops here, Col. Iverson of the 20th Regiment is in command of this encampment and Major Heddrick of the Fort, they think there is no probability of an attack here shortly. 10 miles below us on the river is Smithville, the county site [seat] of Brunswick; just below is Fort Caswell. Our duties are becoming more arduous. I have just received an order directing the detail of 10 new noncommissioned officers and 1 Lieut. to perform picket duty covering a space of 12 miles and not to return to camp for 3 days. Jink, Bennett and McElrath are the noncommissioned officers and Kincaid commissioned they are in good spirits and seem to regard it as a mere excursion. I am glad to hear

Mary is boarding with you (as you say) she will be a great deal of company for you, give her my love and tell her I hope she will become a good churchwoman, we can hear nothing of the movement of Burnside or the intention of our troops said to be 25 Regiments at Kinston, Col. Iverson thinks Burnside will attack them, if so I think he will get a thrashing. You must not be uneasy about me but have faith that God will preserve me to return once more to the arms of my dear Wife and Children. Tell Mag & George I have not rec'd their promised letters yet, I received a package of seed by Winn from Stanley which I sent to Mr. Saunders. There is not a drop of liquor in our camp now, and the Police regulations are so strict that it is almost impossible for the soldiers to get any. The Capt. (Howard) of the Cavalry Company who left these quarters the night we reached here was about to be court martialed for drunkenness, and resigned in order to avoid it, this warning will have a good effect on some of my own. We get the mail every day from Wilmington by my own couriers, so you will continue to direct your letters as before. I am very glad to hear poor Sister has become reconciled somewhat to her sad misfortune. I know it is hard to bear but how much better than the 1st report she will surely appreciate give her my love and tell her to have confidence in Him who orders all for the best. Can't you persuade Ma to ride out and see you occasionally I am sure it would do her and you both good. I am surprised to hear the report about Vance's Regt, it is believed here by all that they fought with distinguished gallantry. I regret to hear that Mrs. Roberts failed to escape from New Bern, altho' I doubt if there is a woman in the Southern Confederacy who will be or is better adapted to foil and hold at defiance the Vandal Yankees than she. What does Mr. Roberts think of it, let me know if he hears from her, it would give me great pleasure to be so situated that I could strike a blow for her release. I esteem her very highly, I hope William will rent the house to one or the other of the parties applying it will go to ruin unless occupied. Tell Stanley to pay Winn's wife $20 he has placed the money in my hands. Jink says give all his love and he will send you his daguerreotype the 1st opportunity he has of going to Wilmington, and I will send you my own if you insist upon it. If you have an opportunity a little Butter will be very acceptable we have been out for 4 or 5 days and it is impossible to get any here. Stanley has not acknowledged check, sent by me to him by Perkins & Bristol. Write more about the children, their sayings and doings. Kiss them all for me and tell Hugh he must not forget (?) and Billy (?). Does Florence still kiss for me? Tell Tillie I will send her a better book next time; is Lucy as full of fun as ever? I would like a little of it this morning; are the services of the church well attended now. Tell George he must sit in my place and remember to behave himself well. Tell Wm. to pay Miss Kate whatever amount of my Rutherford funds he has in her hands, present my regards to her and give my love to all my dear relatives. I know you remember me in your prayers my own dear Wife. God preserve and bless you.

Yours devotedly,

T. Geo. Walton"

Camp Heddrick April 2d/63

My dear Wife,

      I received your welcome letter last night and enjoyed it very much I hope the next will come sooner and be longer. You will see from the station this is dated from, that we have left our old quarters, we left on last Sunday afternoon at ½ past 4 Oclk P.M. and reached here at 10. Oclk P.M. a distance of 20 miles, over a heavy sand road, I felt very reluctant to leave our old quarters after having done so much work in order to make ourselves comfortable, but am very well satisfied with the change, so far as I am personally concerned; The Officers have very nice comfortable quarters, and more satisfactory than all, I have a room to myself which can be kept clean and private when I desire it. This Camp is situated on the Cape Fear about 4 miles from Fort Fisher and 1 mile from the Ocean, I have not been to the Fort but understand it is very strong, having 6 heavy casemated or bomb proof Guns and 24 not casemated there are about 1800 or 2000 troops here, Col. Iverson of the 28th Regiment is in command of this encampment and Major Heddrick of the Fort, they think there is no probability of an attack here shortly. 10 miles below us on the river is Smithville, the county site of Brunswick, just below is Fort Caswell. Our duties are becoming more arduous, I have just recd an order directing the detail of 10 men 3 non commissioned officers & 1 Lieut to perform picket duty covering a space of 12 miles and not to return to camp for 3 days Sink, Bennett & Meblath are the non commissioned officers & Kincaid commissioned, they are in good spirits and seem

Camp Wyatt

April 9th, 1862

"My dear Wife,

I made Jink answer Mag's [Margaret Tilghman Walton] letter immediately, I have not received one from you since but hope I shall to day. I have not left the Camp since we came here, it is twenty miles to Wilmington and I do not know when I shall have an opportunity of going there. I am under the immediate command of Col. Iverson of the 20th Regt. and have not the control of my time as when you were with me. We have just received the news of the Glorious Victory achieved by Johnston & Beauregard in Tennessee [Battle of Shiloh, April 6th], a few more such and the dark cloud which has recently lowered upon us will vanish and the Vandals of the North will be forced to ask for peace. It is believed that very few of the whole Federal force will escape amounting to 35,000. This will enable us to get back all the prisoners they have of ours and a number to spare. I suppose you will have rec'd by the papers all the details before this reaches you. I will send you the Journal the 1st time I go to Wilmington. I do not think there is much prospect of a fight here at present altho' the Yankee Vessels are frequently seen lying off out of range of the guns of Fort Fisher. 5 passed within sight on yesterday. The defenses here I think very good there are 29 heavy guns in Fort Fisher and the batteries adjoining six of them casemated or bomb proof.

The Fort is immediately on the beach of the ocean about ½ mile from the river, just across the Inlet (commanding it) is Zeke's Island with a battery of 11 guns about 3 miles up the river on the Brunswick side is another battery mounting 10 guns and a long line of entrenchments this was originally the site of the old town of Brunswick burned by the British, the walls of an old English church are still standing, within the walls trees are growing two feet in diameter. I crossed the river in a boat yesterday to see it. I learned while there that an old acquaintance Dr. John Hill lived only 2 miles off. I think I will go to see him the 1st leisure day and get a good dinner. We are living pretty hard about now, and I am getting very tired of fried meat and rye coffee. If Hugh Tate comes down try and send me a box by him with some butter & cheese. Tell George one of my men bought a fine turkey, and as we were going to practice at target shooting 100 yards, offhand he proposed that the best shot should have the turkey, and I won, very nearly striking the center. Our men are elated with the anticipation of a good dinner off of him next Sunday. It is strange dear Wife that you and I should be suffering at precisely the same time with severe cold. I don't think I ever had so severe a one in all my life before. I am now however much better, in fact almost well and I have not been confined to my room at all. I am anxious to hear that you have entirely recovered, and if I do not get a letter to day will be uneasy. I have heard nothing from Tom McEntire since he left I suppose he will be here shortly, let me know if he has been to Burke. This is a very unpleasant day heavy wind with rain since midnight. I don't see that vegetation is at all more advanced here than it usually is at home at this season, this is a very desolate region occupied entirely by Pilot and Fishermen the land is scarcely tilled at all, and there seems to be but little difference so far as appearance goes between the seasons, evergreens being the principal growth and the ceaseless roar of the ocean being always the same. I paid Mr. Saunders my bill it was very moderate only $8. The Kincaids paid Ivy $13 apiece. I am sure I never paid a bill more cheerfully and feel very grateful for their kindness to us. I hope dear Wife it will not be long before I can come and see you and all my dear friends. I believe with you that the war will end before the year is out, but not with a subjugated South, this cannot be, we would be unworthy of our birthright was it so. Our cause is just and I have faith that God will answer the prayers of his people which are daily made for the success of our arms; I miss the services of the church here very much, there is a chaplain in the Regt but he has not preached since I have been here, he is a Methodist. Tell Mr. Roberts he has never written me the promised letter about the jug. The water here is very bad and I should be sorely tempted to mix it occasionally if I had the means of doing so, but I think the whiskey blockade much more effectual than the Lincolns, jesting aside if you send me a box tell Stanley to put in a flask to be used in sickness. My command are all well except Laxton [Dr. Joseph Lavender Laxton] who is quite sick with chills. I fear he will not be able to render much service this summer. I do not like this locality much and hope we will be sent some somewhere else before the warm weather begins. I am glad to hear Eliza and her babe are doing well. If you want money tell Stanley to let you have it, tell him to get a statement from Mr. Erwin of the amount I have in Bank, say to Mr. Stacy to get in every foot of land he thinks will make corn. His son has been a little unwell but is better. Tell Florence I want to see her very much, your next letter must be a long one everything about home is doubly interesting to me now. It is almost time for the couriers to start and I must close this uninteresting sheet was it not that it conveys to my dear sweet wife the intelligence of the health and unabated love of her husband.

T. Geo. Walton

P.S. Give my love to all my dear friends & relatives. I have not rec'd a letter from any one of them except you & my children since I left home.

TGW"

TALES FROM A CIVIL WAR PLANTATION

Camp Wyatt
April 9th 1862

My dear Wife,

I made quick answer [to] Mag's letter immediately, I have not received one from you since but hope I shall to day, I have not left the Camp since we came here, it is twenty miles to Wilmington and I do not know when I shall have an opportunity of going there, I am under the immediate command of Col Jarrett of the 28th Regt and have not the control of my time as when you was with me, We have just received the news of the Glorious Victory achieved by Johnston & Beauregard in Tennessee a few more such and the dark cloud which has recently lowered upon us will vanish, and the Vandals of the north will be forced to ask for peace, It is believed that very few of the whole Federal force will escape amounting to 35000, this will enable us to get back all the prisoners they have of ours and a number to spare, I suppose you will have read by the papers all the details before this reaches you, I will send you the Journal the 1st time I go to Wilmington; I do not think there is much prospect of a fight here at present although the Yankee Vessels are frequently seen lying off out of range of the guns of Fort Fisher, 5 passed within sight on yesterday, The defences here I think very good there are 29 heavy guns in Fort Fisher and the batteries adjoining six of them case mated or bomb proof, The Fort is immediately on the beach of the Ocean about ½ mile from the river, just across the Inlet (commanding it) is Zekes Island with a battery of 4 guns

88

The following is a transcription of a letter written by Colonel Walton to his cousin, Mrs. Jessie Webb. The original letter, in very frail condition, is among the historic papers at Creekside, and was written five years before his death:

Creekside, near Morganton, N.C

Febry 1st 1900 A.D.

"My Dear Cousin,

. . . The rent seventy dollars for the Walton Land came to hand in due time and all interested are thankful for the good management and supervision of the premises by yourself. I receive many letters from Tennessee, Pennsylvania, and other points, one recently from Germantown wanting to know about the descendants of the Flemmings of South Carolina. I must decline to respond, one reason why I do so my memory of past events is failing a consequence of old age, I must therefore ask you to do me the favor of referring anyone interested in the ancestors of the Walton family to you being comparatively young, so intelligent and well posted will respond satisfactorily.

Your father knew a great deal about the Virginia branch being a native to the "Manor Born" no doubt frequently spoke to his children of his ancestry and impressed upon their minds the importance of remembering the historical origin of the Waltons of Virginia, and other States of the Union, viz.: Georgia, New York and Pennsylvania, and now my dear Cousin with your assent all persons writing to me about the Walton's will be referred to you, and in order that you may be possessed of the origin of the name Walton and other matters connected therewith which you may not have heard or have forgotten:

Some interesting incidents of the origin of the name Walton a surname of which the Christian name is prefixed occurred long before the Crusades at a Walled Town, high on the Thames River, England elected to aide in the defense of the Town against the assaults of Robbers and Foreigners; and designated as Walton-on-the-Thames; so you see without doubt the name of our ancestors is of long standing and all who bear this name by birth or intermarriage have coursing in their veins some of the blood of this ancient family.

The Waltons who came to the Colonies before the War of the Revolution were very tenacious in clinging to their Christian names, which have been and still being adhered to for more than two centuries, viz: George, John, Thomas, Tilghman, Jessie and William, there are five including myself named George in North Carolina. The Walton family in the United States must be marked by a peculiar physiognomy, illustrating this:

Some years since I saw the celebrated picture in the Capitol at Washington of the signers of the Declaration of Independence, called by Randolph the "leg picture." I at once recognized the portrait of George Walton from his striking resemblance to our family, another illustration more marked if possible, walking on one of the principal streets of the city of Philadelphia, and wanting some hardware, on a sign over the door was inscribed "William Walton, Hardware." I entered the store (impulsively) and found a man whom I recognized at once as a gentleman, he looked at me so attentively that I was surprised, at length having paid for my purchases, he said, "I hope you will not think me impertinent if I ask you your name, "Certainly not it is the same as yours, Walton, "Yes," he said, "I can tell one of them wherever I see him."

Being in Augusta, Georgia (sixty years since) where I met your half-brother, Cousin Alfred, he introduced me to one of the wealthiest men as a relative of ours. "Oh, yes!" he said, "the Walton's are all related." His name was Thomas Walton a great great grandson of the signer of the Declaration of Independence.

. . . Hoping that you may be interested in what I have written and preserve it as it may be of much benefit in years to come to all the Waltons. With much love to you and all my relatives,

I am your affectionate cousin,

T. Geo. Walton"

The following is a letter from Governor Zebulon B. Vance to President Jefferson Davis supporting the nomination of John Walton for Cadet made by Burgess Sidney Gaither of Burke County:

"State of North Carolina
Executive Department
Raleigh Sept. 27, 1863

His Excellency President Davis

Dear Sir,

I beg leave to second, warmly, the nomination of John M. Walton for the appointment of Cadet from N.C. made by Hon. B.S. Gaither, representative in Congress from the 9th district.

This youth is now a private in the 41st N.C.T. (Cavalry) is about 18 years of age and has been in the service since the beginning of the war, proving himself all the time an excellent soldier. He has also had some training at our state military schools.

I do not think a more proper or acceptable appointment could be made.

Very respectfully

Yr. obt. svt. [Your obedient servant]

Z.B. Vance [Zebulon Baird Vance, Governor of N.C.]"

Governor Zebulon Baird Vance, the Civil War
Governor of North Carolina. Photograph:
Library of Congress, Julian Vannerson.

The following letter is a recommendation of John Walton as a Cadet for the 9th Congressional District. It is signed by Representatives and Senators from North Carolina to the Confederate Congress:

"Richmond

April 8th, 1863

His Excellency Jefferson Davis, President (?)

The act of the Provisional Congress of the 16th May 1861 provides that the President shall be authorized to appoint Cadets from the several states, in numbers proportioned to their representation in the House of Representatives and ten in addition (?). There having been no appointment of a cadet for the 9th Congressional District in North Carolina heretofore made, that we are informed of, we take the liberty of recommending John M. Walton of Burke County in said district for the appointment. He is a young gentleman of education, of good (?) and health, fine moral character, and habits, nineteen years of age, was (?) his education at a military school when the war commenced, but soon thereafter abandoned the school, joined the 1st Regiment of North Carolina (known as the Bethel Regiment), and when the time of service of that Regiment expired he joined a cavalry company which had been raised by his father Capt. Walton, known as the Davis Dragoons, and is in service now as a member of that company. From what we know and have been informed of his character and paper record, we take pleasure in presenting his name to your favorable consideration.

In case your Excellency shall please to appoint Mr. Walton, he would he pleased to be attached to the 33rd Regiment, of North Carolina, commanded by Col. C.M. Avery, who is a near relative of Mr. Walton.

We have the honor to be (?):

Wm. T. Dortch [Confederate State Senator, 1st and 2nd Congress].]

Geo. Davis [Confederate State Senator, 1st Congress]

B.S. Gaither [Representative to 1st and 2ndConfederate Congress]

O.R. Kenan [Representative to 1st Confederate Congress]

A.H. Armington [Representative to 1st Confederate Congress]]

R.R. Bridgers [Representative to 1st and 2ndConfederate Congress]

Tho. S. Ashe [Representative to 1st Confederate Congress]

J.R. McLean [Representative to 1stConfederate Congress]

Tho. D. McDowell [Representative to 1st Confederate Congress]]

A.T. Davidson [Representative to 1st Confederate Congress]"

Colonel Clarke Moulton Avery was the brother-in-law of Colonel Thomas George Walton, married to his sister Elizabeth Tilghman Walton (Avery). A letter of recommendation on behalf of John Murphy Walton from Colonel Avery follows. It is not clear to whom this letter is addressed, and the writing on the accompanying envelope is so faint it is now indecipherable:

"33d Regiment N.C.T. [North Carolina Troops]

April 15th, 1863

My Dear Sir,

Yours of the 6th just has been received. J.M. Walton was in the school of Brig. Genl. Jenkins in Yorkville, So. Carolina for twelve months, he was afterwards with Col. Lew at Hillsboro for two years. Upon the breaking out of the war he joined my company in the 6th N.C. Regiment (Bethel) and served six months. He was detailed by the Col. (?) for a good part of the time to drill recruits.

In every position to which he was assigned he exhibited great energy and efficiency.

After the (Bethel) Regt. was disbanded he joined the Davis Dragoons of which his Father T.G. Walton was Captain. He is now a member of this Company. He is eighteen years old. Be pleased to urge his appointment upon the President and ask that he be assigned to the 33d Regiment N.C. Troops. Let me hear from you at your earliest convenience.

Yours truly,

C.M. Avery [Clarke Moulton Avery]"

Photographed document: Rebel Archives, Records
Division of the War Department, Washington, D.C.

Another letter of recommendation for John M. Walton was sent to President Jefferson Davis from William Waightstill Avery: Avery served in the North Carolina House of Commons, the North Carolina Senate and later as Speaker of the House:

"Morganton, N.C.

Sept. 26th, 1863

To His Excellency Jefferson Davis,

Dear Sir,

My young friend John Walton was recommended by Hon. B.S. Gaither, N.C. as a Cadet from his District: I take great pleasure in concurring in that recommendation. Mr. Walton attended the best military schools we had in the South for two years before active hostilities began, and shortly after the commencement of the war whilst hardly sixteen years of age he entered the military service of the C.S. and is now on active duty in the Cavalry Regiment commanded by Col. (?) stationed near Blackwater: Mr. Walton is a young man of intelligence & respectability and desires to continue in the military service after the consummation of the war, and hence he and his friends are anxious that he should secure the appointment of Cadet.

Very Respectfully

Your Obdt. Servant

W.W. Avery"

Letter from Waightstill Avery to President Jefferson Davis, p.1
Photographed document: Rebel Archives, Records Division of
the War Department, Washington, D.C.

Letter from Waightstill Avery to President Jefferson Davis, p.2
Photographed document: Rebel Archives, Records Division of
the War Department, Washington, D.C.

The document below permitted Colonel Walton to travel across North Carolina after the surrender. Though the original document is partially destroyed, it was signed by P.C. Hayes, a Lieutenant Colonel and Provost Marshal General of the Army of the Ohio, commanded by Major General John Schofield. Photographed document: Private collection of family.

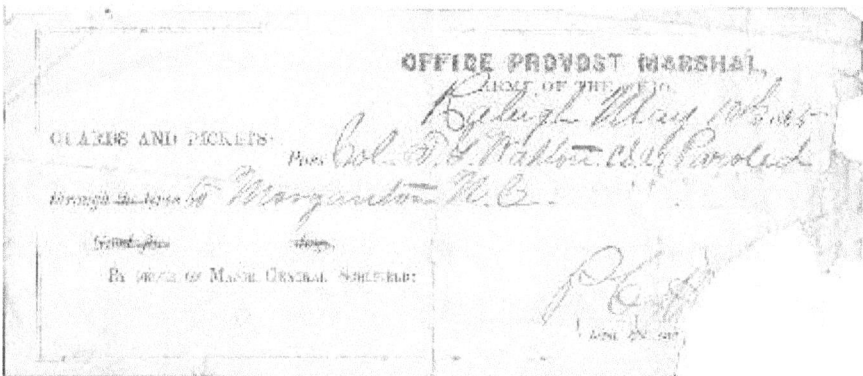

The Oath of Allegiance to the Government of the United States signed by Colonel Walton is transcribed as follows:

"OFFICE PROVOST MARSHAL GENERAL,

(ARMY OF THE OHIO.)

Raleigh, N.C., May 10th, 1865.

In accordance with the terms of the Military Convention entered into on the twenty-sixth day of April, 1865, between General Joseph E. Johnston Commanding the Confederate Army, and Major General W.T. Sherman, Commanding the United States Army in North Carolina, Col. T. G. Walton, 8th N.C. Home Guard, has given his solemn obligation not to take up arms against the Government of the United States until properly released from this obligation; and is permitted to return to his home, not to be disturbed by the United States authorities so long as he observe this obligation and obey the laws in force where he may reside.

Sworn and subscribed to before me, this Tenth day of May 1865.

T. Geo. Walton
Col.

P. C. Hayes
Lieut. Col. and Provost Marshall General,
Army of the Ohio."

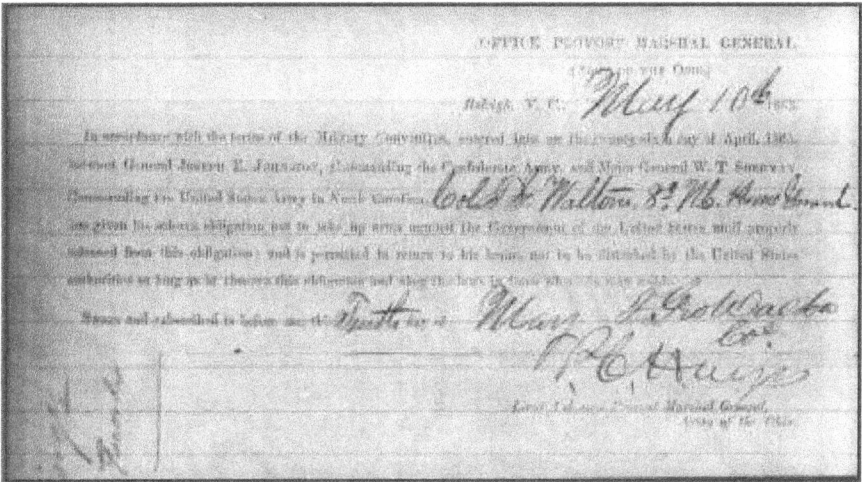

Oath of Allegiance.
Photographed document: Private collection of family.

Creekside. Photograph: Library of Congress,
Frances Benjamin Johnston, 1939.

The following is a transcription of Colonel Walton's Amnesty Papers requesting pardon from President Andrew Johnson. Colonel Walton was excluded from the general pardon granted to southerners whose financial worth was less than $20,000. In October 1865, he traveled to the White House to procure a presidential pardon from Andrew Johnson:

"Burke County, N.C.

13th July 1865

To His Excellency
President Andrew Johnson.
President of the United States.

The petition of Thomas G. Walton of the County of Burke and State of North Carolina respectfully showeth to your Excellency, that he is a native born citizen of the County of Burke and State of North Carolina, that for many years he has taken an active part in the politics of the Country and has always cooperated actively with what was known as the Whig party. That he has always opposed publicly with whatever ability he had the doctrine of secession, and in the beginning of the year 1861 when an effort was made in North Carolina to call a Convention for the purpose of taking the State out of the Union he zealously canvassed the County of Burke in opposition to the scheme and to thwart the designs of the secessionists and partly owing to his efforts the Convention scheme was voted down in the State at the first election. He further shows that he never was a believer in the doctrine of secession and never prior to the passage of the ordinance of secession by the Convention in May 1861 voted for any person for any political office who advocated or favored the doctrine. After North Carolina was declared no longer a member of the United States by the Convention, he then as a matter of necessity and because he had no other alternative did co-operate with his State in endeavoring to gain a separate independence for the so called Confederate States and upon the office of Colonel of the Home Guard of Burke Co the 8th Regiment composed of the Counties of Burke, Caldwell and McDowell being tendered to him by the Governor of the State, he accepted said appointment and endeavored in good faith to discharge all the duties which devolved upon him by virtue of his said office, to this extent and no other has he acted for the interests of the so called Confederate States and against that of the United States.

Your petitioner would further show that he is included in the 13th Section of the excepted cases in your Excellency's proclamation of the 29th May 1865.

Your petitioner being willing and anxious to return to his allegiance to the United States Government and to cooperate with all good and loyal citizens in restoring the authority of the United States in the State of North Carolina and in restoring law and order throughout our limits would most respectfully ask your Excellency to grant to him a full and free pardon for all his offences and to extend to him such other further relief in the premises as your Excellency may seem expedient and as the merits of his care may require and as in duty bound your petitioner will ever pray.

T. Geo. Walton

State of North Carolina, Burke County"

Colonel Walton's Amnesty Papers. Photographed
document: Rebel Archives, Records Division, War
Department, Washington,D.C

The following letter from Tod R. Caldwell to William W. Holden is appended to Colonel Walton's letter of amnesty. Caldwell and Walton were boyhood friends, both from Morganton, and would remain friends throughout life. As the first Lieutenant Governor of North Carolina, Caldwell would take the office of Governor upon the impeachment of William W. Holden after the Civil War:

"State of North Carolina

Burke County

William W. Holden

Prov: Govt. of North Carolina

I hereby certify that I am personally and well acquainted with the foregoing petitioner Thomas G. Walton and that I have every reason to believe and do believe the facts set forth in his said petition to be true and I therefore recommend him to your Excellency's favorable consideration.

13th July 1865   Tod R. Caldwell"

The following document is attached to Colonel Walton's Amnesty Papers and requires that he swear to defend the Constitution and support the emancipation of slaves:

"State of North Carolina.

Burke County.

I, Thomas G. Walton do solemnly swear or affirm, in presence of Almighty God, that I will henceforth faithfully support, protect, and defend the Constitution of the United States, and the Union of the States thereunder; and that I will in like manner abide by and faithfully support all laws and proclamations which have been made during the existing rebellion with reference to the emancipation of slaves. So help me God.

T. Geo. Walton
Sworn and subscribed to before me, this the 13th day of July A.D. 1866

[Signed] Tod R. Caldwell
Col. and Aide to His Excellency
W.W. Holden Prov: Govt. N.C."

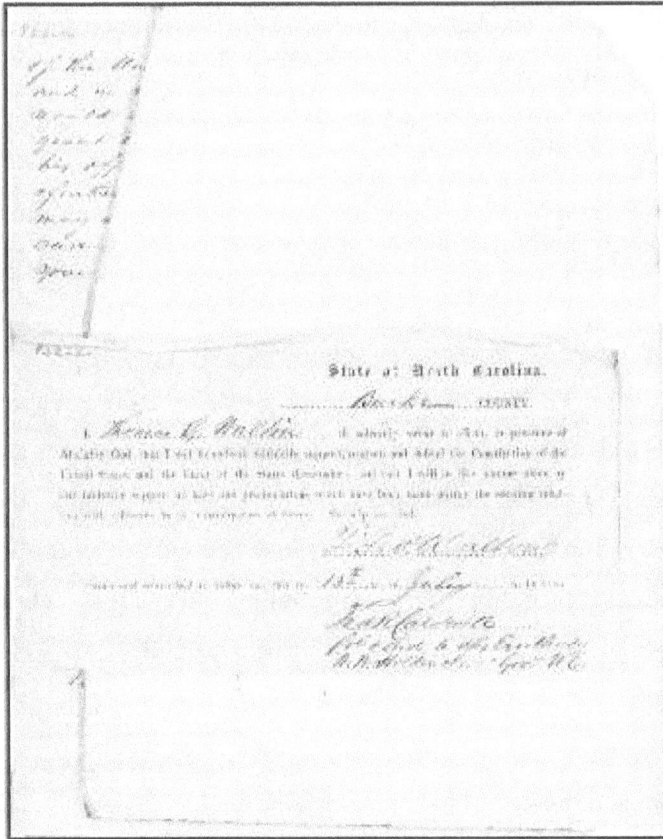

Colonel Walton's oath to defend the Constitution of
The United States, support all federal laws, and respect
the emancipation of slaves. The document is signed by
his friend, Governor Tod Caldwell of Morganton.
Photographed document: Rebel Archives, Records
Division of the War Department, Washington, D.C.

A signed and sealed stock certificate from the Western North Carolina Rail Road Company to Colonel Walton is transcribed below. Colonel Walton was a Director of the Western North Carolina Rail Road Company.

"WESTERN NORTH CAROLINA RAIL ROAD COMPANY

No. 159.   50 Shares

Be it known that Thomas Walton of Burke is entitled to Fifty shares in the Western North Carolina Rail Road Company, transferable by the said Thos. Walton either personally or by Attorney only at the Office and on the books of said Company.

Witness R.C. Pearson President of the said Western North Carolina Rail Road Company, at Statesville under the seal of the Corporation, this 12th day of Mch, 1859.

A. F. Simonton   R. C. Pearson
Secretary   President

SHARES $100 EACH."

\

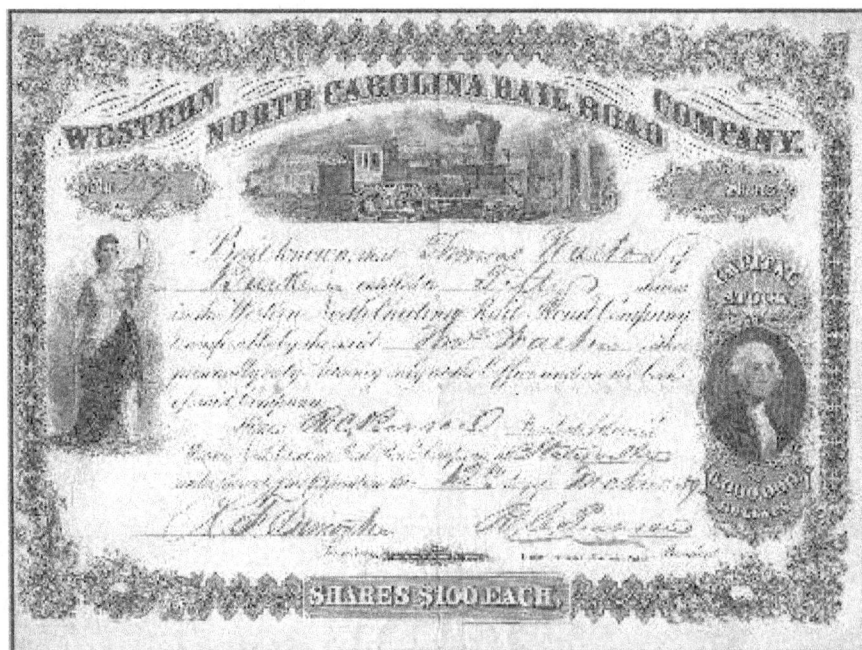

Stock certificate in the Western North Carolina Railroad
Company. Colonel Walton was one of its Directors.
Photographed document: Private collection of family.

A transcription of the medical diploma of Dr. John Alfred Walton, brother of Colonel Walton, upon his graduation from the Medical College of South Carolina, reads:

"MEDICAL COLLEGE
OF THE
STATE OF SOUTH CAROLINA
CHARLESTON, 16, S. C.

OFFICE OF THE DEAN

TO ALL TO WHOM THIS DOCUMENT MAY COME:

We the President, Vice-President, and Professors of the Medical College, at Charleston, in South Carolina witness and by these presents certify that after an assigned and fixed demonstration of sciences, skill and practice, we admit John A. Walton, N.C., to our order and confer on him the Degree of Doctor of Medicine, to enjoy its rights and privileges.

In testimony whereof we set our hands and seals in this document.

Johannes Edward Holbrook, M.D.   Thomas Y. Simmons,
President   Anatomy Professor.
Jas Ramsay. M.D., Surgery   J.M. Campbell, M.D.,
                                  Vice-President

Saml. H. Dickson, M.D.,   Jas. de la Motta, M.D., Senb.
    Practice of Medicine
Henry R. Frost, M.D., Materia Medica
Edmund Ravenel. M.D., Chemistry
Thomas G. Frioleau, M.D., Obsts.
Stephen Elliott, M.D., Botany"

The following is a letter from Colonel Walton to Clara Cheesborough on the occasion of her engagement to Herbert Huske Walton, 1898:

"October 31st, 1898

My dear Clara,

I cannot express by writing my deep, unfeigned gratification, at the strong proof Herbert has given of his wisdom as well as love, in selecting one for his wife so endeared to all his relatives, here by family ties. With the assurance, that you will meet with a warm welcome by all who have Walton blood in their veins; with wishes that your future life may be crowned with love and happiness,

I am with esteem and affection your Uncle,
Miss Clara Cheseboro.'   T. Geo. Walton"

Barreksville,
Oct. 31st 1898

My dear Laura,

I cannot express by writing my deep, unfeigned and affection, at the strength of intellect Herbert has given of his wisdom in... in selecting one for his wife so endeared to all his relations, here by family ties. With the assurance, that you will meet with a warm welcome by all who have Walton blood in their veins. With wishes that your future life may be crowned with love and happiness. I am with esteem and affection your

Aunt,

Miss Laura ....

The Old Kitchen

7. FOOD IN THE OLD SOUTH

The variety and abundance of food consumed on the southern plantation of the 19th century varied greatly according to social position. The food consumed by slaves and their overseers, differed greatly from the daily fare of the planter family. Simple daily rations of items such as peanuts, black-eyed peas, cornmeal cakes and salt pork were common fare for slaves. Occasionally, whiskey or rum was provided during times of celebration.

A soldier in the Confederacy, prior to 1863, ate cornmeal cakes, dried peas, salt pork or bacon, peanuts, dried apples, molasses, sugar and fresh vegetables when available. Coffee or tea was drunk. After 1863, when the ravages of war had rendered food scarce to families all over the South, Confederate soldiers received only a handful of peanuts and a couple of strips of salt pork or bacon daily on which to march and fight. Hardtack, a rock hard type of cracker, was generally eaten by Union troops, and though disparaged as inedible by both sides, it was confiscated by Confederate soldiers from dead or captured enemies as a food source. Food might be foraged from farms, though this was forbidden by Southern commanders. General Lee required Confederate soldiers to pay for the food they were given. Near the end of the war, however, when troops were starving, commanders turned their heads and many soldiers crawled through fields to find sweet potatoes. Coffee was no longer available because of blockades, so soldiers used chicory and sometimes ground peanuts or rye to make coffee. A lucky soldier might discover a packet of coffee on the body of a dead Union soldier after battle. Hunger and dysentery were rampant.

Tales of Union and Confederate sentries calling temporary truces in order to exchange food, commodities and conversations abound. The most typical exchanges involved Confederates trading tobacco with Union troops in exchange for real coffee. Other items sought included newspapers and sewing notions such as needles and buttons.

In the early years of the war, 1861-1862, conditions for prisoners on both sides were adequate, because the food supply was sufficient and the numbers of prisoners were relatively few. As the war dragged on, however, the scarcity of food increased and the price of food rose exponentially. Huge numbers of starving prisoners confined to inadequate housing spread disease. The horrific tales of Union prisoners dying in Confederate prison camps in large numbers fueled the anger of the Union toward the South during the war and remained a source of contention long after.

In truth, the shocking number of deaths was, in part, a reflection of the widespread starvation being experienced across the entire South—starvation caused by blockades, poor transportation, the shortage of men available to work the land, plant and tend crops, and the destruction by Union armies of food supplies in the South.

A variety of crops were grown across the Old South including contributions introduced by African slaves, the culinary traditions of Native Americans, and foods of Caribbean origin which found their way to the United States through the slave trade. Items originally brought by slaves to the New World include okra, watermelon, cowpeas or black-eyed peas, peanuts, sweet potatoes and sorghum. Yams, which are not related to sweet potatoes, though the two are often confused, are tubers grown in the Caribbean and South America. Sweet potatoes, rather than yams, were the food crop of the south. Peanuts were originally from South America, but found their way to African slaves through Portuguese slave traders and eventually to the fields and tables of the Old South. Peanuts were one of the foods given to African slaves on the passage from Africa to the New World.

Prior to the Civil War, food was plentiful on southern plantations. According to cookbooks of the time, a variety of foods were available: fresh, salted and smoked meats from domestic sources, wild game, fish and shellfish; breads, buns, biscuits and rolls made from rice, buckwheat, cornmeal and wheat flours; layer cakes, pound cakes, fruit cakes, tarts and puddings; pecan, molasses and fruit pies; a variety of beers made from hops, ginger, and spruce, and wines made from blackberry, apple, cherry, grape and elderberry; a variety of jams, jellies, marmalades and preserves made from blackberries, crabapples, apples, oranges, plums, watermelons and peaches. Ice cream was made from a variety of fruits, coffee and chocolate. Vegetable dishes were numerous, and soups were made from ingredients as diverse as oysters or peanuts, depending upon the particular area of the south. Liquor made from corn or rye was popular. Condiments made on the plantation included ketchup, yeast, molasses, salad dressings, relish and mayonnaise.

Curious recipes from the Old South abound, particularly since the custom of writing down recipes is fairly modern; historically, recipes were transmitted verbally across generations. As a side note, Early Americans, including those in the Old South used the word "receipt" rather than "recipe." This custom was probably derived from settlers who came over from Great Britain.

One curious recipe comes from "Creekside Family Receipts" a collection of family recipes compiled in 1973 by my aunt, Ariail Boggs Wood, from a number of family recipes which date from the Civil War to the early 1900s. This recipe comes from Clara Patton Murphy who was Colonel Walton's sister-in-law. The recipe in its original wording reads as follows:

Aunty's Mince Meat

"Boil a pig's face until very tender and cut it up fine. To this add the same quantity each of apple, raisins and currants—sugar, of course, and as much citron as you like; all well-spiced and the whole covered with whiskey."

Another curious recipe is taken from an addendum to the family recipe book by Jean Cameron Poland including footnotes which advise the reader to leave out part of the recipe in order to improve it. It should also be noted that giving exact measurements was not important at that time:

Turkish Delight

½ box of gelatin soaked in enough water to cover it

2 cups of granulated sugar

¼ tumbler of cold water

Grated rind and juice of one orange

When water and sugar come to a simmer add gelatin and orange and let boil well 20 minutes. Add nuts and fruits. Then pour in a shallow wet pan to harden overnight. Cut in squares and roll in powdered sugar. Walnuts, coconut and raisins are nice. (Note: Coconut would be nasty. This is from

Uncle Smith. Cousin Florence's daughter, Cameron, says add rum or brandy or whiskey—maybe nuts, but not raisins or coconut.)

Note the use of lard in the following recipe for ginger snaps (which includes a list of ingredients but no instructions). In modern times, lard has become very unpopular in food preparation because of health concerns.

Not only the use of lard, but the amount of lard used in this recipe will raise modern eyebrows:

Ginger Snaps

1 cup molasses

1 cup of sugar

1 cup of lard

½ cup of water

1 tablespoonful of ginger

1 teaspoon of cloves

1 teaspoonful of soda

Enough flour to roll

It should be noted that many fine recipes exist in "Creekside Family Receipts," including the family recipe for fruitcake which was brought over from England when the family emigrated from Walton-on-Thames in the 1600s. This recipe is closely guarded, however, along with the plum pudding recipe which was always served at Christmas dinner with a sprig of holly stuck in it. Prior to serving the dining room lights would be turned off and the plum pudding covered in brandy, lit, and ceremoniously brought to the holiday table. Interestingly, the family recipe for fruitcake, which includes over nine pounds of preserved fruit and laborious preparation, ends with this simple directive, "Bake awhile."

An amusing footnote to this tale involves my grandmother and her love of the family fruitcake. Prior to the holiday season at Creekside, fruitcakes were made which would last through Christmas and into the New Year. After the fruitcakes were baked and carefully wrapped, they were stored for a time to allow the flavor to develop. One year, my grandmother quietly stole into the dining room where the fruitcakes were stored and scooped out pieces of cake from the underside. She repeated this ritual daily until she had worked her way around the entire fruitcake, tunneling it out and leaving only a shell. When the time came to cut the Christmas fruitcake, the family was astonished to see that it was completely hollow.

The spinning wheel also known as a "walking wheel,"
used for spinning wool while standing."

Old Toby Jugs from a tavern in Scotland.

LOUISA EMMONS

The Ice House as it looks today. It appears as a depression filled with brush in the middle of the photograph. Photograph by Alex Emmons.

8. THE ICE HOUSE

At the time of the Civil War, food preservation consisted of canning, salting, drying, smoking, pickling, curing and fermenting. These methods were all used in North Carolina and throughout the South.

Creekside, in those days, had a smoke house which was located in the back yard not far from the kitchen. Meat heavily salted for preservation was hung in the smokehouse. The heat inside the smokehouse, combined with a large quantity of salt, caused the walls to become saturated with salt. Pigeons pecked the mortar of the smokehouse in order to procure the salt, and this caused the deterioration of the building which no longer exists.

Since the kitchen and the smokehouse both made use of open fires, they were placed away from the main house. This practice was customary in the south and prevented the main house from absorbing excessive heat during the summer months which were often hot and humid. It also reduced the possibility of fires to the main house. The danger of fire was ever present in Civil War days because of the widespread use of fireplaces for cooking and warmth. Though the kitchen at Creekside is attached to the main house, it is located in another wing which stands perpendicular to the main house.

Keeping food cold was a more difficult proposition in those days. Those fortunate enough to have a spring on their property often enclosed a portion of the spring to create a springhouse in which items such as butter and milk were laid in a kind of trough over which the flowing water ran. This kept the food chilled to the natural temperature of the water.

Another method for cold preservation was the ice house. At Creekside, the ice house was located in the woods behind the house. It consisted of a hole of approximately 12 feet across and possibly 10 feet deep. These are approximations based upon the current dimensions of the ice house, but it is certain that it was once both wider and deeper than today. The old ice house is currently covered over with trailing ivy, but it remains a deep depression sometimes used as a place to toss rotting tree limbs and dead bushes. Though there is no longer a covering over the ice house, it is likely that a wooden structure resembling a small house once covered the depression since this was the custom during the days when ice houses were common.

The method for maintaining the ice house was universal during the 1800s. Blocks of ice were used to fill it, and large quantities of sawdust were shoveled over the top, preventing significant melting even into the summer months. Silver Creek, which runs alongside what is now the Greenway in Morganton, was the source for the ice. It was from this creek that blocks of ice were carved with saws and transported by wagon to Creekside during the winter months. The ice house was an ingenious method for chilling butter, milk and cheese. It also provided ice for drinks, making ice cream, and for cooling fevers.

The "Yankee Bench," a Union camp bed left behind in 1865.

A portrait of James Willie Young Walton (1805-1842),
older brother of Thomas George Walton, painted by
Thomas Sully. Property of family.

9. A BONE AND A BUTTON

The truth about old houses is that they change over time. Old structures are converted to make way for modern conveniences. As a house built without indoor plumbing, it became necessary, over time, to convert the existing structures in Creekside to accommodate indoor toiletry. Fortunately, the closets that were once built to accommodate 19th century fashion, also served well for 20th century bathrooms.

Wide brick panels set into the ground, known as "carriage stops," can be found at the foot of the steps on either side of Creekside's pillared front porch. They have not changed over time, but they serve no purpose now for there are no longer any horse-drawn carriages which arrive and depart. The carriages and horses of yesterday have given way to automobiles and driveways, and the carriage stop of past centuries has become a garage. The modern era is more convenient, but not very romantic.

The elegance of the 19th century parlor with its formal fireplace and murals, lace curtains, piano and chandelier, remains, though the silences are long and deep in a room once designed for polite conversation; when to "parler" meant simply to talk, another disappearing art in an age of texting, emails and television.

The new heart of the family home has become the kitchen, rather than the dining room, and perhaps this is in keeping with an age of informality when day to day gatherings no longer involve the rigorous planning and execution of yesteryear when even breakfast was a formal event.

Sometimes the very existence of the old trappings gives way to change, and they pass away altogether: at Creekside, the smokehouse is long gone, the well has been filled in, and the ice house is slowly being reclaimed by nature. The hole that was the opening to a root cellar accessible from inside the house has been covered over.

One curious tale told by my uncle, Herbert Walton Boggs, known as "Sonny", and now deceased, relates how as a boy he enjoyed climbing down into the root cellar under the house to explore. The entrance to the root cellar, which was called the "potato hole" by family members, was located in a closet within the dining room. It consisted of a hole in the wooden floor through which root vegetables were dumped onto the dirt floor of the cellar below. The cold, dark environment of the root cellar preserved vegetables for extended periods of time. Potatoes, carrots and onions were stored in this fashion to provide food during the winter months.

On one of these forays down through the dark spidery potato hole, Sonny discovered two objects—a human femur and a button from a Yankee uniform. The only conclusion the family could derive from this was that a Union soldier, perhaps a deserter, had wandered onto the property with questionable motives and been disposed of and his body hidden in the root cellar. Alternatively, a violent incident might have occurred during the Federal occupation, and the family, fearing retribution from the enemy, quickly hid the body from sight. No one living has an answer to this mystery, but clearly the body was removed at some point and two incriminating objects were left behind. My uncle kept the button, though it has been lost over time. The current location of the femur remains a mystery.

III. CIVIL WAR GHOSTS

Grave of John Murphy Walton (1844-1872).

10. A GHOSTLY CONFEDERATE SOLDIER

In the 1940s, my mother, Mary Boggs and her sister Ariail, shared one of the upstairs bedrooms in Creekside. At this time, radiators were used as a heat source, and the old fireplaces which existed in every room of the house remained unlit except on rare occasions.

One night, Ariail was awakened by the sound of footsteps, and she sat up in bed. Beside the unlit fireplace, she saw a Confederate soldier standing in profile, dressed in uniform and wearing an officer's hat. He turned to look at her, and terrified, she frantically tried to awaken her sister. Refusing to be awakened, Mary slept soundlessly through the ghostly incident, but Ariail broke out in hives from the experience and was in such a state of terror she was unable to go to school the next day.

Interestingly, my grandmother, Louse Walton Boggs, had seen this same apparition many years earlier, when a young woman. Being an only child, she frequently sought out the company of friends from school. She had invited a group of young women over to Creekside for the night during her college days at St. Mary's Episcopal College in Raleigh. They stayed in the bedroom adjoining the one where Ariail and Mary would sleep years later. This bedroom was known as the Blue Room because of its color scheme. A bathroom, converted from an original closet, separated the two bedrooms. My grandmother and her friends laughed and talked late into the night, when suddenly, a ghostly Confederate soldier drifted through the closed door and into the room. The girls screamed repeatedly until Louise's father, Herbert Walton, came racing upstairs and threw open the door, shouting, "By jolly, what's going on here!" Between terrified gasps, they related the incident of the ghostly apparition to him. As a side note, Herbert Walton was never known to curse and, therefore, his use of the term "by jolly" was probably the closest he ever came to uttering foul language.

Who was this ghostly Confederate soldier? And why, so many years after the war, was he unable to rest in peace? Some have speculated that it was the ghost of John Walton who had escaped capture at Appomattox and made his way home, a distance of 250 miles, only to die a young man of twenty-seven of the tuberculosis he had contracted during the war.

The final chapter in this ghostly tale involves my then future husband, Kirk Emmons, who was a friend of my grandmother's before I was ever introduced to him. He came to visit my grandmother one summer in the 1970s and was assigned to the Blue Room upstairs. During the night, he awoke and was startled to see the profile of a man's head, shoulders and chest in Confederate uniform and officer's hat gliding silently across the bedroom from the door to the window. The spirit paused briefly near the foot of the bed while looking toward the window, and then moved on, quietly disappearing into the darkness before reaching the window.

11. A TORMENTED SPIRIT

I borrow this tale from my grandmother's unpublished book, "Tales of Creekside: Historical and Supernatural:"

"The Greenlees were the first owners of the plantation purchased in the early 1830s by Colonel T.G. Walton. Their slave graveyard was back of the big Creekside barn that sat on the hill on the east side of the house...Old Aunt Harriet, born a slave herself, would stand by those graves, each marked by a plain unmarked stone, no doubt put there by the Negroes."

"The old kitchen at the end of the Creekside ell, has a basement and chimney original with the former house, and dates 1783. When I was a child, the cooking was done on an old black iron cook stove. At night, a chimneyless oil lamp lighted it. It sat on a corner shelf, and I often watched the black smoke rising from it."

"Aunt" Harriet retired immediately after supper, going to her basement room below the kitchen. Jane remained to wash the dishes in a huge tin dishpan...I stayed with her. Her chores done, she said, 'Now baby I'se got to count the silver. I'll be back directly.' Shortly after her departure, I began to hear a mournful and distant sound coming from near the big barn. It drew nearer and nearer, a dreadful screaming sound, the most sorrowful and woe-begone I've ever heard. It sounded as one might imagine a soul in torment. It was a bright night with the yard outside the kitchen window bathed in moonlight. As I looked out the window, I could plainly see the old well, and the dreadful screams drew ever nearer. Suddenly, I saw the unhappy ghost itself It was white---not just plain white but luminous, and its head turned from side to side, as it paused near the well. The voice was human, high-pitched like a woman's, [and] the shape of the creature was animal-like, [but] neither dog, sheep nor cow. Presently, it walked down the old rock road headed toward Silver Creek, and the screams echoed in the distance."

"I rushed to the dining room to join my mother and Jane. 'I've seen a ghost,' I said. 'Didn't you hear it screaming?' They had not. I've never seen the ghost again, but I've awakened from a deep sleep and heard it a number of times. The dreadful screams are always the same, and my blood runs cold when I hear them. Will that poor, tormented soul never find peace? Several members of my family have also heard it, but only I have seen this apparition."

I include this tale told by my grandmother for several reasons. First of all, my grandmother, born in 1899, provides valuable, first-hand, written documentation of a bygone era which she experienced. There is no piece of researched history as useful and as revealing as an account told in the first person narrative by an observer. Secondly, old houses such as Creekside bear old memories of sorrowful and turbulent times, and sometimes they give witness to the strange events of the past. My grandmother was particularly sensitive to such occurrences, and the tales she told of the unexplainable are as much a part of the history of the house as any piece of historical research.

Thirdly, I include this tale because I am one of the family members who heard the mournful cries of the apparition.

I lay in the bed at Creekside as a young child, not yet asleep, and I heard that terrifying, inhuman wail rise up out of the darkness. Chills ran up and down my body as I listened, and I was paralyzed with fear. The agonized wailing sound rose up and down, and it seemed to move swiftly across the yard and die away as it moved on. The sound must be similar to the cries of that legendary creature, the Banshee, whose wailing presages coming death. I have no explanation for the sound, nor do I wish to contemplate its meaning even after all these years, but as far as I know it has not been heard in about 50 years. Perhaps that anguished soul has found rest at last.

12. THE UNEXPLAINED

Every room at Creekside has a tale to tell, particularly the bedrooms, and most rooms have had ghostly visitors whose presence has been attested to by family members over the years. Some family members have been more sensitive to the presence of the otherworldly than others, particularly my grandmother who seemed to have a "gift" for seeing spirits, as does my son. My aunt Ariail always had a kind of sixth sense about the presence of spirits, and I have heard sounds over the years that have no reasonable explanation.

My mother has a very early recollection of a ghostly visitor. As a young child, she slept in the bed her father had made for the Boggs children. This bed was placed in the Blue Room near her parent's bed. She remembers waking up during the night feeling cold, and seeing a gentle smiling woman with a radiant glow all around her. The woman stood by the bed and smiled down at her. Reaching down gently, she pulled the covers up around my mother. When my mother told my grandmother about the ghostly visitor, my grandmother told her it must have been the spirit of Clara Cheesborough Walton, my mother's grandmother.

Another visitation involving Clara Cheesborough Walton took place when my grandmother and grandfather left for the beach for a week with their six children.

After World War II, my grandfather bought a defunct Coast Guard Station at Murrells Inlet, South Carolina. The station was actually a house that stood out in the inlet on pilings, and family members had to reach it by boat. On this vacation, the family had left Herbert Huske Walton behind at Creekside, in the care of Roscoe Huskins, his caregiver. When they returned from South Carolina, Roscoe said, "That woman sure did play some pretty music." My grandmother asked what he was talking about. "That woman in the parlor sure did play some pretty music on that piano," he said. Clara Cheesborough Walton had been an accomplished musician and had often played the piano in the parlor. She had died in 1935.

As a child, I enjoyed playing the piano in the parlor, but I never went in that room that I did not have an uncomfortable feeling about being there. There was just an eerie feeling in there as if I were being observed. On one occasion when I was sitting at that piano, I heard a loud hissing sound like the sound of steam coming from the radiator to my right. At that time, radiators were still in all the rooms at Creekside though they were no longer in use; natural gas lines had been installed in the 1960s. I quickly rose from the piano stool and walked out of the parlor, though I very much wanted to run.

When I was a child, family members came up to stay at Creekside every year during the Christmas holiday, and this was always a wonderful time. In early years, the large Christmas tree was always in the hall outside the dining room, so tall it reached up into the upper story. The smell of evergreen filled the downstairs. Late in the evening, close to midnight, one of my uncles, feeling restless and unable to sleep, went downstairs to the kitchen to make a cup of coffee. As he walked down the main flight of stairs in the silent house, he heard footsteps following behind him. Every step he took, he heard a step behind him. The experience greatly unnerved him. He related the incident in the morning and declared that he was now a confirmed believer in the supernatural.

My grandmother used to sleep in one of the upstairs bedrooms known as the Children's Room. One morning, when she came down to breakfast, she said she had heard a dog underneath her bed panting during the night. There had been no dog present in that room. When my son was a young child and we were visiting my parents at Creekside, he went upstairs by himself to the same Children's Room and was startled to see the family hobby horse near the window rocking by itself.

Many members of the family have heard the sound of footsteps in the Blue Room upstairs. The footsteps are only heard when one is in the living room below, and they slowly move back and forth across the room, creaking the floorboards as they walk.

Other ghostly tales from Creekside are not so benign. The Yellow Room, a bedroom located on the second floor of the house, has always given family members an eerie feeling. When my great aunt Marie Boggs Hickey and her mother Kate Archer Ariail Boggs stayed in that room on a visit to Creekside in the 1940s, the covers were rudely jerked off of them to the foot of the bed during the night.

An incident took place downstairs in the master bedroom where I slept as a young child when I lived at Creekside for a few years. The fear generated by this incident remained with me for many years. I had woken up while it was still dark outside and was lying in the bed very early in the morning, before sunrise. I wasn't thinking about anything in particular, but I suddenly received a very hard slap in the face. I was terrified, and did not even move. I was absolutely frozen in fear. I lay there until the sun came up before I was willing to move. I have no explanation for that event, but I actually thought long and hard about whether I really wanted to move back into Creekside in 2009; the incident disturbed me that much.

When I first moved into Creekside with my husband and son, I experienced a strange phenomenon. We had all retired for the night, but my husband and I were still awake. I heard a very loud crash in the downstairs hall, and immediately said, "What in the world was that?" Neither my husband nor I had any idea what it could have been, but since the security alarm was on, we were not worried about intruders. I assumed a picture had fallen off the wall and crashed to the floor. Not really wanting to go check it out at that moment, we both agreed we would find out what happened in the morning. When I went downstairs in the morning, nothing was out of place, no pictures had fallen, and there were no signs of disturbance anywhere.

In 2012, a similar incident happened again, but I was the only one to hear it. The incident took place on a weekend, early in the morning. My husband had gone downstairs to feed the cats, and my son was still in his bedroom. Our bedroom and my son's bedroom share a bathroom which is located between them. I was in the bathroom fixing my hair when I heard loud stomping footsteps in my son's room. It sounded like someone was deliberately stomping around angrily. I said loudly to my son, "What are you doing in there?" At that moment, I heard a tremendous crash in his room that sounded like the shattering of glass and china as if it were being thrown to the floor. I went racing around to his bedroom door, since he keeps the bathroom door locked on his side. I threw his door open. He was sound asleep. "Didn't you hear that?" I cried out. He was totally oblivious and still half asleep. He had never heard a thing. Nothing in his room was disturbed.

In her later years when my grandmother no longer liked to climb up and down the stairs, she slept in the old wing of the house that was part of the pre-Revolutionary foundation upon which Creekside was built. My grandmother was a very brave person, unafraid of anything, certainly not afraid of anything in her home place. She related a terrifying incident that she had experienced during the night. While lying in her bed late at night, she had seen a woman with an evil face approaching her bed. My grandmother cried out to the apparition, "You go away and leave me alone!" and she prayed hard. The apparition disappeared.

IV. LIFE AFTER THE WAR

Louise Walton Cheesborough.
Photograph: Private collection of family.

Herbert Huske Walton and Clara Cheesborough Walton.
Photograph: Private collection of family.

13. THE NEXT GENERATION

Much of the South had undergone brutal punishment during the War: poverty, hunger, the death of family members and friends, the destruction of homes, the taking of personal property and the final bitterness of defeat and repatriation. The South was scarcely prepared for reconciliation since its enthusiasm for victory had never adequately prepared it for defeat. It came as a shock to many that the Confederate States of America was no more. The bitter days of Reconstruction lay ahead.

Land was resurveyed and deeds were rerecorded where courthouse records had been burned, family trees were rewritten where family bibles were lost, the slow process of rebuilding bridges, railroads and other public works began, all in a nation on the verge of bankruptcy from four shockingly brutal years of war. The rebuilding of personal lives was not as easy. It is estimated that 600,000 lives had been lost in the war. Entire families had been wiped out, and the suffering of civilians was intense and personal. No one in the South escaped the horrors brought to their own doorstep. It was to be the healing of the heart that would be the greatest test of the South during Reconstruction and long after.

The government of the United States set about providing for the reunification of confederate states. Troops were planted in every state in the South to ensure that the laws in force were upheld. A special set of laws were enacted to ensure the peace during this period and to maintain the newly reunited southern states.

Two companies of troops from Ohio were stationed in Morganton during this time in order to protect local citizens from carpetbaggers and other opportunists who roamed about the South during Reconstruction to make their fortunes. They were also stationed to assure that the rights of freed slaves were upheld. Apparently, the Ohioans were well received and at least two of their officers intermarried with local women.

Herbert Huske Walton, born August 25, 1860, was the youngest child of Colonel Walton and his wife, Eliza Murphy. Named for the first Episcopal rector ordained at Grace Episcopal Church, the Reverend Joseph Caldwell Huske, Herbert Walton was the handsomest of the Walton men. Born just eight months before the start of the Civil War, he was a small child when his two older brothers, James and John, left home to fight in the war with their father.

Herbert was married to Lola Kirkland in 1888, and a male child was born from that union who was named Samuel Kirkland Walton. The child succumbed at the age of two, only two months after the death of his mother in 1891, and is buried in Grace Episcopal churchyard along with his mother. Herbert then married Evelyn Erwin (1879-1897) who died in childbirth. No children were born from that union, and Evelyn is buried at Forest Hill Cemetery in Morganton. Herbert's third wife was Clara Cheesborough, his second cousin.

Though he was married three times, Herbert Walton had always been in love with Clara Cheesborough of Asheville and asked her to marry him before proposing to each of his other two wives. She turned him down twice, but when he asked Clara a third time, she was in her thirties and finally consented. A warm letter of welcome was sent to her from her future father-in-law, Colonel Walton, praising Herbert's good sense. At the age of forty, Clara gave birth to a female child who was named Louisa Anne Cheesborough Walton, later changed from Louisa to Louise.

A Republican, like his father before him, Herbert voted at the Burke County Courthouse regularly on Election Day, but his wife was unable to exercise the same privilege since the vote for women had not yet been realized. Women's suffrage in the United States had begun in the 1830s, and shortly after the Civil War, the issues of black suffrage and women's suffrage began to be linked together. Though the 13th Amendment abolished slavery, and the 15th Amendment granted the vote to black males, it was not until the 19th Amendment that the voting privilege for women was adopted, and the amendment was ratified in 1920. At that time, Herbert's wife Clara exercised her privilege to vote and expressed her tendency toward independence. She voted as a Democrat, unlike her husband, and when she met him on the steps of the courthouse on Election Day, she declared, "Mr. Walton, I have come to cancel out your vote."

Herbert continued in the tradition of a gentleman farmer after the Civil war. Though tracts of land had been sold off during difficult financial times, and slave labor had ceased to exist, he continued to farm the land at Creekside. Corn and rye were the primary cash crops grown while beans, sweet potatoes, onions, carrots, peas and other smaller volume crops were grown for family food. Herbert's efforts as a farmer were a great success. He entered his crop of mountain rye in a competition at the International Exhibition (also known as the World's Fair) in Chicago in 1893.

The International Exhibition was a celebration of the 400th anniversary of Columbus' arrival in America. The city of Chicago was chosen from a number of competitors in order to showcase its dramatic resurrection two decades after the devastating fire that consumed much of the downtown area on October 10, 1871. The fire was termed the Great Chicago Fire because of the devastation it inflicted including the burning of 2,000 acres in the heart of the city and the loss of 300 lives.

Herbert received an award and a medal at the age of 33 for the yield, weight, and color of his crop of mountain rye. The award, which hangs at Creekside, reads:

THE UNITED STATES OF AMERICA
BY ACT OF THEIR CONGRESS HAVE AUTHORIZED
THE WORLD'S COLUMBIAN COMMISSION

At The International Exhibition Held In The City Of Chicago, State Of Illinois In The Year 1893, To Decree A Medal For Specific Merit Which Is Set Below Over The Name Of An Individual Judge Acting As An Examiner, Upon The Finding Of A Board Of International Judges, To

H.H. WALTON *** MORGANTON

NORTH CAROLINA.

EXHIBIT: MOUNTAIN RYE

AWARD

FOR FOOD YIELD, WEIGHT AND COLOR.

YIELD, 25 BUSHELS PER ACRE.

WEIGHT, 56 ½ POUNDS PER BUSHEL.

H.D. Pritchfield
President Departmental Committee

Geo. B. Davis
(?)

T.W. Palmer
Vice-President, World's Columbian
Commission

Geo. H. Park
Individual Judge

John Boyd Thacher
Chairman, Executive
Committee of Awards

Jno.T.D. Kinson
Secretary, World's
Columbian Commission

Herbert took part in the census after the war. To accomplish this, he had to locate the remote cabins of mountaineers who lived along the far boundaries of the county. In the mountains of North Carolina, it was always advisable to call out when approaching a cabin since moonshine stills were fiercely protected and the presence of strangers was not appreciated. Upon approaching one mountain cabin, he called out and was met at the door by a surprisingly polite mountain man who invited him in and even offered him a cup of coffee. At that time sugar, also known as "short sweetening," was not plentiful and many people resorted to molasses, or "long sweetening" for their desserts and drinks. Herbert's polite host served his cup of coffee to him and asked, "Will you have long sweetenin' or short sweetenin'?" Pleasantly surprised at the offer and greatly heartened by the thought of a cup of coffee with real sugar in it, Herbert replied heartily, "Why, I'll have short sweetening, thank you!" "Sorry, we haint none," came the laconic reply. Apparently, it didn't hurt to offer.

Herbert smoked a corncob pipe and enjoyed dancing a jig. He was an avid hunter and fisherman and accomplished at both, though my aunt Eliza Cheesborough Boggs Kirk remembers that he would never bait his own hook and always took hired help along with him to provide this service. Pictures at Creekside show Herbert with parties of hunters from the north that he would lead on expeditions into the mountains. On one of these expeditions, he killed a large black bear, skinned it, and made a rug out of it. It lay on the floor of the upstairs bedroom occupied by his grandson, Herbert "Sonny" Boggs, who liked to dress up and roam around in the bearskin from time to time. Sonny's hound dog slept on the floor of his bedroom on the bearskin rug until it became infested with fleas and had to be tossed out.

Herbert's grandchildren remember their childhood at Creekside fondly. Their father, Harry Boggs, constructed a child-sized train and laid a train track from the top of the hill at 819 West Union Street where a field was then located, down to the bottom of the hill at the back yard of Creekside. The train had a smokestack made from a metal stovepipe, and the date when it was constructed, 1934, was the number of the train. The children would hop on the train, standing up and holding onto the side, and it would run down the track by gravity. When it reached the end, it had to be pushed back up the track again.

He also built a white wooden colonial style dollhouse for the two youngest children, Eliza and Florence. The dollhouse had an upper and lower floor and stood beneath a small pine tree in the back yard. One could climb inside by crouching down and going through the front door. I remember the dollhouse from my childhood, though it no longer exists.

In his old age, Herbert had a caregiver named Roscoe Huskins, a local man, who tended to him. Roscoe was born with a deformed foot and spent a great deal of time wrapping and rewrapping it with rags to cushion it from rubbing against his shoe. Roscoe had limited mental capacity, and though capable of performing the duties for which he was hired, he was somewhat childlike. Both he and Herbert walked with canes and from time to time would engage in cane fights.

Herbert Walton and his daughter, Louise, enjoyed antique hunting together and purchased several pieces of furniture and china that remain in the house today. Louise adored her father, and when she married Harry Boggs, an architect from Birmingham, Alabama, they continued to live at Creekside and take care of Herbert in his old age. For his birthday, his

The train built by Harry Boggs for his children.
Front to back: Herbert "Sonny" Boggs, Mary Murphy Boggs,
Clara Katherine Boggs. Photograph: Private collection of family.

daughter always gave Herbert the largest can of Prince Albert tobacco that could be purchased, and he kept an apple in the can to flavor his tobacco.

One of their favorite pastimes was setting up a card table in the downstairs hall at Creekside where the sun streamed through the window onto the landing and down into the hall. While Herbert, Harry and Louise played poker at the table, Herbert's two oldest grandchildren, Sonny and Clara, would collect moths and other bugs from the windowsill and put them in their grandfather's hat. When he put his hat on, dead bugs would rain down on his head. In retaliation, Herbert would give them "Indian pinches" by grabbing a piece of skin on their arm or leg and giving it a twist. When younger sisters Eliza and Florence would stare at Herbert in silence, put off by his aged appearance, he would deliver the same pinches to them.

On one occasion, the Episcopal bishop came to visit, and my grandmother and grandfather served him refreshments in the parlor. Sonny and Clara disappeared mysteriously during the visit. When it came time for the bishop to leave, he looked about for his hat. Other family members began to search also, with mounting dread, noting the absence of Sonny and Clara. The Bishop's hat was located upside down by the holly tree near the driveway, filled with sand. Sonny and Clara had used it as a scoop to pour sand into the bishop's radiator. A hose had to be brought to wash out the sand and my grandmother and grandfather apologized profusely. The Bishop shook his hat out with dignity and placed it quietly on his head. He never visited again.

Florence Septima Boggs and Eliza Cheesborough Boggs in the yard at Creekside. Photograph: Private collection of family.

Marie Ariail Boggs, Clara Katherine Boggs and Mary Murphy Boggs
on the back porch at Creekside. Photograph: Private collection of family.

Louise Cheesborough Walton as a young child.

Photograph: Private collection of family.

14. THE HORSE TROUGH

Colonel Walton, among the members of his household, was the undisputed head of the family and warranted great respect. He was born in an era when the head of the household was an autocrat who loved his family but held high expectations for all its members.

His granddaughter, Louise, as a child did not yet fall under the scrutiny of her grandfather and spent her childhood days doing pretty much as she pleased. Her days were spent playing among the household staff in the kitchen, sitting on the milk jugs on the back porch swinging her legs, and running around the yard unfettered. Though she knew her grandfather, her youthful spirits had not yet fallen under his piercing blue gaze.

I remember my grandmother laughing as she related this tale:

"My mother, Clara Cheesborough Walton had decided that I was to start joining the family in the dining room on Sundays rather than eating with the kitchen staff as I always had. Sunday dinner was a formal affair at that time. After visiting Grace Episcopal Church, the family returned home and sat down to dinner dressed in their Sunday best with the Colonel at the head of the table."

"I remember very well my mother laying out a frilly white dress for the occasion. I was carefully dressed and my hair was brushed into place and a ribbon tied in it. I decided to take one last walk down the back steps. I remember hearing the busy hum of talk from the kitchen and the odor of Sunday dinner being prepared as if drifted out to me. It was an early spring morning and a light crisp wind gently blew the frills of my dress around me. The ribbon in my hair fluttered slightly in the breeze."

The Colonel often enjoyed walking around the yard in the morning, surveying the lovely home he had created for his family. Cool green vines climbed up the walls of the majestic house and four mighty white columns supported the front. The house gave the appearance of being able to withstand any hardship, and indeed, it had seen many.

As the Colonel rounded the corner, lost in reverie, little Louise was surveying the horse trough in the back yard, mesmerized by the moving reflection of the water and its dark shifting undulations created by the light wind. The sweet, sad memories of childhood, now moving swiftly beyond her reach, flashed across her mind, and with one mighty heave, she joyfully leapt into the horse trough. She said she remembered the frills of her white dress floating lazily across the top of the water. She also remembered the feeling of great abandonment and freedom as she turned in the horse trough and met the curious gaze of her grandfather. With scarcely a second glance, he lifted his head, turned silently away and walked on. She did not dine with the family that Sunday.

Glen Alpine Springs Hotel, built by Colonel Thomas
George Walton in 1878. Photograph by permission
of *Picture Burke*, Burke County Public Library,
Morganton, NC.

15. GLEN ALPINE SPRINGS HOTEL

Built by Colonel Walton in 1878, and located near Brindletown in Burke County, Glen Alpine Springs Hotel was the largest frame building in North Carolina. Colonel Walton and his son-in-law, John Pearson, were the proprietors. I include this wonderfully descriptive tale told by my grandmother, Louise Walton Boggs, because it is a colorful and fine piece of writing, and because it relates the anecdotal history of Glen Alpine Springs Hotel.

A Short Sketch about Glen Alpine Springs Hotel

(as remembered by T.G. Walton's descendants)

"In a mountain nook, quiet and secluded even in the busy twentieth century rush, lie a few piles of rock, part of a fallen chimney and an old stone wall--all that remains of the once gay and popular Glen Alpine Springs Hotel. The mineral springs were first discovered by Colonel Moulton Avery, father of the late I.T. Avery, and he found the mountain cove at once so cool and delightful and beautiful a spot that he erected a cottage and spent many happy weeks there with his family."

"After the turmoil and devastation of the Civil War, Colonel T.G. Walton, dreamed of a gathering place in which people would be cheered, benefited in health and gain a new and cheerful view of their lives still shattered by the disheartening result of the war. Such a dream grew in magnitude until it came into being from an English architect's pencil---one Charles Collier. The building was erected with an expenditure of thirty thousand dollars ($30,000). Begun in 1876, it was completed in 1877. It contained fifty rooms all comfortably and tastefully furnished. One entered an immense lobby which by night grew into the ballroom, where the gay and lighthearted ladies and gallants danced the Lancers and Virginia Reel, interspersed with occasional waltzes. This room was lighted with four large kerosene chandeliers, each containing four lamps. As the evening grew in gaiety, the gentlemen walked downstairs to the bar below where could be bought the finest of wines, French brandies and all manner of liquor. The parlor was the "room of many windows." It stood in the tower and was plastered white with walnut trim in the English fashion. The dining room contained two large chandeliers and smaller lights on either side of each and every window. This room measured 40 x 50 feet and here elegant meals were served with much of the food...being sent from New York."

"A promenade on top of the roof ran the entire length of the hotel and on fine nights the Negro orchestra repaired to it and the dances were held under moonlight and starlight in the very shadow of the mountains against which the hotel nestled. For amusement, the guests had a billiard and pool room, a ten pin alley and croquet was enjoyed on the huge lawn, which swept under towering oaks and spruces almost out of sight. A homemade flying jenny likewise graced this lawn with seats instead of horses. The rooms in the hotel were spacious and comfortable, and the wide front piazza delightful to rest on and view the beautiful surrounding country. The stairway was unusual in that the banister rails were alternating maple and walnut."

"The hotel boasted three springs---the Temple one, a lovely affair with a huge soapstone bowl, had lythia [probably lithium] and alum minerals, one down a steep ferny incline was sulphur, and still further was a cool delicious, tasteless pool perhaps containing a little iron, but known as the "Free-Stone Spring."

"There were eight cabins for the exclusive mortals who preferred to be far from the noise of the dance and the smell of frying chicken. Some of these were built by private individuals, one being Neilson Falls, the first (grandfather of Buck Falls). He and his wife resided there every summer. Some cabins had two rooms and some just one. Three mountains rose directly behind and to the sides of the hotel---Monte Crucis was so named because a giant spruce which was in the exact shape of a cross grew on its summit, Propst Knob, the highest peak in the South Mountains and Cyst Gap."

"A hack drawn by four horses met the train at Glen Alpine Station (name changed from Turkey Tail to that of the hotel by Col. Walton) daily. This was nine miles from the hotel and quite a journey in those days. The train brought guests from as far east as Wilmington and as far west as Old Fort. Those coming from Asheville had to come by stage coach to Old Fort."

"Glen Alpine Springs operated as a hotel until 1900, was later sold and used as a mountain school, then abandoned until it nearly rotted down, then burned up about six years later, it is said, from a bootleg still."

The register for Glen Alpine Springs Hotel remains at Creekside, and is dated from July 17, 1878 to August 16, 1897. The last entry shows Colonel Walton and his son Herbert Huske Walton staying for dinner at the Hotel on August 16, 1897.

The facing page of the hotel register is covered in 19th century graffiti—stamped postmarks from the Hotel, initials written in the script of the time, quick mathematical equations jotted down, and random doodles which serve no apparent purpose other than to permit a bored clerk to pass the time.

Elsewhere in the register, the heading "Sunday, Sept 8th (1875)" has been artfully converted so that the letters in each word mimic small snakes complete with scales and forked tongues. Comments jotted in the book in various hands include such entries as, "I took my girl to the fancy ball;" and "You do love me, don't you?" with the biting reply, "I don't care a (unreadable and underlined)." Another entry shows two names bracketed together with the word "lovers" jotted out to the side. On Saturday, August 30th, 1879, the clerk notes, "No animals today" in bold letters. Elsewhere, the picture of a turkey with sparse tail feathers has been sketched with a pencil.

The names of guests at the Glen Alpine Springs Hotel include entries from surrounding states and as far away as New Orleans, New York, London and Africa.

An old postcard of Glen Alpine Springs Hotel.
Private collection of family.

The Flood of 1916. Smith Street, Asheville, NC.
Photograph: Public domain.

16. THE FLOOD OF 1916

Clara Cheesborough Walton, a second cousin of Herbert Huske Walton, was a native of Charleston, South Carolina. When her family heard that Sherman intended to burn Charleston, they fled to a family summer home in the mountains of Asheville, North Carolina, called "Azalea," later relocating to another family home in Asheville, "Springvale," which would become their permanent home. Clara Cheesborough Walton would later become the third wife of Herbert Huske Walton.

The family used Springvale primarily during the summer months when they escaped the dangerous heat and disease of Charleston. Deadly fevers abounded in the Old South, particularly in the semi-tropical areas along the seacoast, and those who were able traveled to cooler climates where the danger of disease was less problematic.

During the time period when Springvale existed, the family employed the father of writer Thomas Wolfe of Asheville. Wolfe's childhood home still stands in downtown Asheville as a tourist site, though it suffered damage from fire in 1998 and underwent renovation.

Springvale was situated on the Swannanoa River beside what is now the Municipal Golf Course in Asheville. It was reached by crossing over a narrow wooden plank bridge supported by iron girders. The river itself had steep banks, cut by cycles of flooding. I can remember visiting Springvale as a very young child. My father got out of the car, and I could see the worry on his face as he surveyed the narrow wooden bridge across which the car would have to travel. His concern conveyed itself to me, and I fearfully looked down at the Swannanoa River over which we passed as the car crawled along to the other bank.

In the early 1900s, Asheville was still a small mountain town, filled with trading posts where Native Americans came down from the Qualla Boundary reservation in Swain County to conduct business. A common custom at that time among Native Americans in the area was to smear their bodies with bear grease during the winter months as a protection against the cold weather. The grease formed a kind of protective insulation. My grandmother remembered visiting some of these trading posts in her childhood and smelling the odor of the bear grease which became rancid over time. It was a powerful smell combined with that of tobacco and the smoky wood stoves which were the heat source in trading posts.

The Flood of 1916 has been well-documented in various publications such as "The Floods of July, 1916," a report by the Southern Railway Company which was written in 1917. Local reports from citizens in Asheville also provide a valuable first-hand account of the terrible destruction of this flood caused by the convergence of several natural events. Stories are told of terrified victims clinging to tree limbs to avoid being swept away by the flood waters.

Days of heavy rains fell in Tennessee and the Carolinas in mid-July of 1916, with 22 inches of rain reported to have fallen at Alta Pass in Mitchell County within the 24 hour period prior to the flood. This tremendous volume of water, combined with two hurricanes, one which hit the Gulf Coast, and the other which touched down in Charleston, South Carolina, had put all the streams of the Tennessee River in flood stage. The ground was said to have been saturated down to the bedrock. These waters swept eastward toward North Carolina, and on the Sunday morning of the flood, citizens awoke to the blowing of the cotton mill whistle and the ringing of the riot call on the fire bell. The alarm had been sounded, but there was scarcely time to seek higher ground before the devastating floodwaters swept through. At final count, the flood waters crested at about 21 feet.

Tremendous damage was incurred, about $22,000,000, according to estimates of the time. At least eighty lives were lost, and many homes and businesses swept away, particularly in the Biltmore Village area of Asheville. Edith Vanderbilt, the widow of George Vanderbilt of Biltmore House, provided relief to the community with financial assistance in the form of food, transportation and blankets.

Family reports from the Cheesboroughs describe the terrifying rise of the Swannanoa River as it swept over the banks and flooded into the dining room of Springvale, rising up until the family fled in fear to the upper floor. The river rose until the furniture went afloat and bumped against the ceiling of the lower floor. Tremendous damage was done to the house which later succumbed to the rot and structural weakening caused by the flood in addition to damage caused by a rare tornado which swept through Buncombe County in the 1970s.

When my grandmother's maiden aunts fled to the upper floor of Springvale for protection, an amazing incident occurred. A Native American in a canoe, searching for victims in distress, paddled by and picked them up out of an upstairs window to take them to higher ground. One can only imagine the picture of two spinster Victorian ladies in the feminine dress of their time, stepping gingerly out of a bedroom window above the turbulent river into a canoe manned by a native Cherokee tribesman. The tale itself is a real piece of Americana which captures that moment when a clash of cultures is briefly reconciled.

My own limited memories of Springvale, though less colorful, provide a similar contrast. They include the flock of white geese that always swam on the river below the house. The family fed the geese, so they regularly appeared on the bright summer lawn, and I remember running fearfully from them toward the grape arbor as they flapped their wings and honked. I fled to the large porch that surrounded one side of the white wooden house, and arrived to see Aunt May in a lace cap serving afternoon tea on the porch. The Victorian house was dark inside, and I remember the shadows under the stairwell where an antique child's chair was kept. I was very intrigued with that chair, and somewhat covetous, because I had never seen a chair made just for a child.

Springvale is now gone, but the iron girders which supported the rickety wooden bridge have, ironically, survived flood and time.

Springvale. Photograph: Private collection of family.

An oil painting of Brookwood by Carlotta Smith Norton. Property of Walton family.

17. THE BURNING OF BROOKWOOD: 1920

Colonel Thomas George Walton and William McEntire Walton were brothers, the sons of Thomas Walton of Charleston, South Carolina, and his wife Martha McEntire Walton.

The Walton brothers married the Murphy sisters of "Willow Hill," a plantation in Burke County: Thomas married Margaret Eliza Murphy in 1837 and William married Harriet Louisa Murphy in 1845. The Walton brothers built plantation houses with adjoining property just west of Morganton. Beautiful Brookwood was a stately white plantation house, its front portico supported by four massive Doric columns, topped by a roof with wooden shingles and situated in a grove of oak trees. Brookwood was located on the property now occupied by the Sigri Great Lakes Carbon Plant. Creekside and Brookwood were practically identical in design except for the materials from which they were constructed--Creekside was a brick house and Brookwood was wooden. This distinction would later prove to be disastrous for Brookwood. Katherine Walton Thomason, the now deceased granddaughter of William McEntire Walton, related some humorous and fascinating accounts of the "Brookwood Waltons" in the second volume of *Burke County Heritage: North Carolina* published by the Burke County Historical Society.

The following is a retelling of one of her recollections of life at Brookwood:

There were no schools during the time when Katherine's father, William Erwin Walton, was a boy so his parents hired a governess to teach the children in a little school house at Brookwood. The children from Creekside sometimes came over to the school for their lessons, too. The teacher, Miss Kate, announced one day that Katherine's father had behaved badly, so she accompanied him to the big house and locked him in an upstairs room, declaring that he would have nothing to eat but bread and water for dinner. After a time, he heard a voice calling up to him and looked out the window to see the family cook, "Aunt" Phronsie. She told him to drop a string down, which he did, and she tied a bucket to it which contained the dinner she had secretly provided for him—chicken, ham and pie. While he was hungrily devouring the meal, he heard Miss Kate coming up the stairs. He hastily stashed the bucket in the closet and threw a pair of old pants over it. Miss Kate unlocked the door and brought in a slice of bread and some water on a tray for him.

Another story related by Katherine Thomason tells of a visit to Brookwood by mounted Union troops. They rode through the big gate and into the lot behind the house. One soldier greeted young William Erwin Walton with "Hello, Johnny Reb!" Another soldier went to draw water while a third soldier took corn from the granary to feed the chickens. As the chickens approached to eat, the soldier would lop their heads off with his sword. Another trooper went down into the potato hole to look for food, and the other soldiers forgot he was there and left him behind when they rode off.

♦ ♦ ♦

My grandmother, Louise Walton Boggs, as a young teacher in Drexel in 1920, was accustomed to riding the train back and forth from her home at Creekside to teach school daily. One afternoon as she rode home, she remembered hearing a loud commotion as the train rounded a curve and approached the hillside which looked down on the wooded areas around Creekside and Brookwood.

"Oh, my God!" came the cry in unison as passengers leapt to their feet, "Brookwood is burning!" The two stately homes were local landmarks, their names known to all. My grandmother remembered staggering to her feet with a sick feeling. The home of her cousins, the "Brookwood Waltons," was on fire.

The fire was said to have been started by burning leaves which blew upward onto the wooden shingles of the roof in the wing where the kitchen was located. The fire rapidly spread across the house, completely destroying the structure and all the furniture except for a few pieces which were rescued and dragged out into the yard. It was a terrible loss for all the family.

The only painting of Brookwood of which I am aware was presented by my mother, Mary Murphy Boggs Alexander, to the late Tom Walton, a prominent Morganton businessman and a direct descendent of William McEntire Walton. The oil painting, probably copied from an old photograph, was by Carlotta Smith Norton, a descendant of both Walton brothers, and it shows a stately white plantation house in a grove of trees with a hunting dog resting in the front yard.

APPENDIX A.
Descendants of Edward Walton (1645-1688)
and Elizabeth Booth (1641-1717)
(including George Walton, Signer of the Declaration of
Independence)

Note: Family members who are underlined indicate the direct line through which Thomas George Walton (1815-1905) descended.

Robert (or John) Walton was an English soldier who emigrated from Walton-on-Thames, in Surrey County, near London. Family tradition says he was one of three younger sons (Robert, George and John) of a Lord Walton, all of whom emigrated when an elder brother received the family inheritance. The family genealogy is difficult to trace prior to the mid-1600s, though oral history persists in the passing on of this tale. The name of Robert's (or John's) spouse is unknown, but he is believed to be the father of Edward Walton, below:

Edward Walton (1645-1688) was a planter, born in New Kent County, Virginia. He married Elizabeth Booth (1641-1717) in 1671 for 5,000 pounds of tobacco.
Children:

Edward Walton (II) (1668-1720) of New Kent County, Virginia
Married Elizabeth Mason (1670-1717).
Children:

1. **Robert Walton** (1692-1733) of New Kent County, Virginia.
Married Frances Sherwood (1697-1780).
Children:
Robert Walton (II) (1717-1750).
    Married Mary Hughes (1723-1760).
    Children:
        a. John Walton (1742-1781).
        b. Robert Walton (III) (1744-1797).
        c. Sarah "Sally" Walton (1746-1805).
        d. George Walton (1749-1804). Signer of the Declaration of Independence for the state of Georgia.

2. **William Walton** (1700-1747). Born in New Kent County, Virginia. Married Susannah Rice Cobb (b. 1702) of New Kent County, Virginia. Sold 400 acres in Albemarle County, Virginia, and moved to Goochland County, Virginia. His will left 2,120 acres on the north and south sides of the James River in Albemarle County to their children. The Walton home and 400 acres on the north side of the James River was left to daughter Frances upon her mother's death.

3. **Mary Walton** (born prior to 1698).

4. **Thomas Walton** (1703-1772) of New Kent County, Virginia. Died in Cumberland County, Virginia.
Married Martha Cox in 1734.

5. **Elizabeth Walton** (1707-). Born in New Kent County, Virginia.
Married Peter Rowlett (d. 1754).

6. **John Walton, M.D.** (1709-1772). Born in New Kent County, Virginia.
Married Mary Sims (1708-1805).

7. Edward Walton (III) (1720-1791).
Married Elizabeth (?) (1723-1775).

8. Martha Walton.
Married George Sims.

APPENDIX B.
Descendants of William Walton (1700-1747) and
Susannah Rice Cobb (1702- ?)

1. **Jesse Walton** (1740-1789). Known as the founder of Jonesboro, Tennessee, in 1778. Elected to the North Carolina Legislature in 1779, he moved to Georgia in 1781 and was killed in a battle with the Cherokees in 1789. Married Mary Walker (1748-1800).

2. **Frances Walton** (b. 1734).
    Married Henry Mullins (1744-1797).

3. **William Walton (II)** (1736-1806). Born in Amherst County, Virginia, he indentured himself to his brother Jesse's guardian, William Coxe at 16. At 19, he sold his inheritance, 300 acres on the north side of the James River in Albemarle County, settled in Goochland County and married Elizabeth Tilghman in 1758. He fought in the Battle of Camden (1780) and the Battle of King's Mountain (1780) in the American Revolution. He settled in Morganton, North Carolina in 1791 with his son William (III). Married Elizabeth Tilghman (1744-1787); daughter of Thomas and Lucy Hix.
    Married Mildred Lavender in 1792.

4. **Susannah Walton**.
Married James Hilton.

5. **Mary Walton**.
Married Absalom Jordan.

6. **Anne Walton**.
Married Charles Cobb.

7. **Louisa Walton**.
Absalom Jordan became her guardian in 1758 until she married Jeremiah Terrell in 1759.

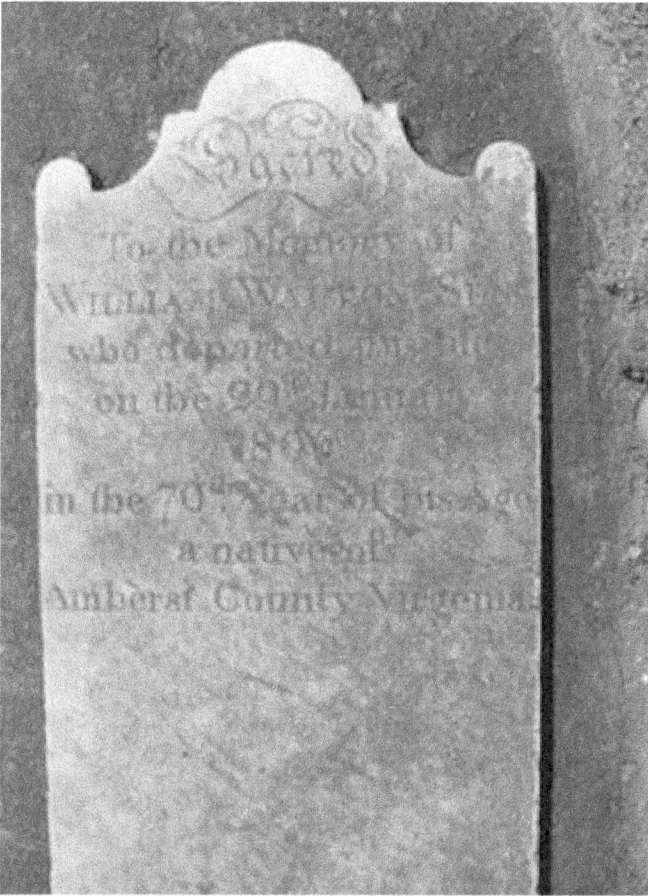

Tombstone of William Walton (II) of Amherst County, Virginia. Both he and his son, William Walton (III) fought at the Battle of Camden (1780) and the Battle of Kings Mountain (1780) in the American Revolution. Father and son moved to Burke County, N.C. after the death of William Walton's (II) wife in 1791. His grave is at the First Presbyterian Church in Morganton, N.C.

Strawberry Hill Plantation, in Greene County, Alabama, was built by William Walton (III) (1767-1844), an uncle of Colonel Thomas George Walton. The above photograph shows Strawberry Hill as it looks today. Photograph in the public domain.

Photograph: Front entrance of Strawberry Hill Plantation in 1936. Library of Congress, Alex Bush.

Photograph: West elevation of Strawberry Hill Plantation in 1936. Library of Congress, Alex Bush.

APPENDIX C.
Descendants of William Walton (II) (1736-1806) and Elizabeth Tilghman (1744-1787)

1. **Tillman Walton** (1760-1831).
Married Judith Walton, cousin. (1770-1846).

2. **William Walton** (1762-1846).

3. **Thomas Walton** (1762-1768).

4. **Jesse Walton** (1766-1766).

5. **William Walton (III)** (1767-1844). Born in Amherst County, Virginia. Impressed into service by Captain William Loving at the age of twelve to mill wheat, corn and oats for the Continental Army of Virginia for twelve months. Joined his father to fight in the Battle of Camden (1780) and the Battle of King's Mountain (1780) in the American Revolution at the age of thirteen. Settled in Morganton, North Carolina in 1791. Lived in Charleston, South Carolina, prior to 1808 and became a merchant in the slave trade. Shipped slaves from the Port of Charleston to his 600 acre plantation located at the mouth of Johns River, Burke County, North Carolina (later owned by Colonel John Sudderth). Here, slaves were taught to speak English and to learn farming methods before being sold.

Built Strawberry Hill Plantation in 1828, a cotton plantation, near Forkland in Greene County, Alabama on 1,000 acres of land. Married Jennie McEntire (1775-1799).
Married Justina Louisa Gennerick (1790-1868).

6. **Elizabeth Walton** (1769-).

7. **Lucy Walton** (1770-1771).

8. **Robert Walton** (1776-1786).

9. **John Walton** (1778-1817).

10. **Polina Walton** (1779-).

11. <u>**Thomas Walton**</u> (1782-1859).
    Married Martha Matilda McEntire (1784-1868).

12. **George Walton** (1773-1835).
    Married Nancy McEntire.

13. **Nancy Walton** (1784-1825).
    Married Amos Davis of South Carolina.

14. **Edmund Walton** (1786-1807).

APPENDIX D.
Descendants of Thomas Walton (1782-1859)and
Martha Matilda McEntire (1784-1868)

1. **James Willie Young Walton** (1805-1842).

2. **John Alfred Walton, M.D.** (1807-1830).

3. **Jane Clarissa (Clara) Walton** (1809-1837).
   Married James Washington Patton (1803-1861).
   Children:
   > James Alfred Patton (born c. 1831-).
   > > Died of disease in a Confederate Army camp.
   > Thomas Walton Patton (born c. 1832-).
   > William Augustus Patton (born c. 1835-).
   > > Died of disease in a Confederate Army camp.
   > John G. Patton (born c. 1836-).

4. **Louisa Anne Nancy Walton** (1811-1844).
   Married Thomas Taylor Patton.
   Children:
   > Martha Ann Patton (1833-).

5. **Martha Matilda Walton** (1814-1850).
   Married William Crawford Erwin (1809-1876).
   Children:
   > Clara Erwin.

Anna Elizabeth Erwin (1841-1909).
Laura Erwin.
Emma Henrietta Erwin (1844-1900).
Ella Matilda Erwin (1849-1926).

6. **Thomas George Walton** (1815-1905).
Founder of the "Creekside Waltons."
Married Margaret Eliza Murphy (1820-1886).
Children:
       Ella Walton (1839-1839).
       Edward "Stanley" Walton (1840-1898).
       James Thomas Walton (1842-1916).
       John Murphy Walton (1844-1872).
       Margaret Tilghman Walton (1848-1917).
       George Walton (1849-1904).
       Lucy Walton (1851-1922).
       Martha Matilda Walton (1852-1936).
       Florence Louise Walton (1855-1930).
       Hugh Collett Walton (1858-1867).
       Herbert Huske Walton (1860-1949).

7. **William McEntire Walton** (1819-1909).
Founder of the "Brookwood Waltons."
Married Harriet Louisa Murphy (1825-1891).
Children:
       Lauretta Elizabeth Walton (1847-1920).
       Thomas Walton (1849-1922).
       William Erwin Walton (1850-1929).
       Adelaide Avery Walton (1852-1921).
       Eliza Murphy Walton (1858-1858).
       Waightstill Avery Walton (1859-1929).
       Tilghman Young Walton (1862-1898).
       Kate Martha Walton (1865-1936).
       Harriet Louise Walton (1867-1944).

8. **Elizabeth Tilghman Walton** (1822-1882).
   Married Clarke Moulton Avery (1819-1864).
   Children:

   Martha Matilda Avery (1844-1916).
   Adelaide Avery (1848-1848).
   Mary Lenoir Avery (1852-1854).
   Isaac Thomas Avery (1856-1941).
   Lizzie Tilghman Avery (1858-1858).

APPENDIX E.

Descendants of Thomas George Walton (1815-1905) and Margaret Eliza Murphy Walton (1820-1886)

1. **Ella Walton** (1839-1839).

2. **Edward "Stanley" Walton** (1840-1898).
   Married Kate Blackwell.
   Children:
   > Lillian Walton Burr Avery (1861-1905).

3. **James ("Jink") Thomas Walton** (1842-1916).
   Married Margaret Erwin McDowell.
   Children:
   > James Thomas Walton, Jr. (1876-1951).
   > Hugh Collett Walton (1869-1877).

4. **John ("Jock") Murphy Walton** (1844-1872). Unmarried.

5. **Margaret Tilghman Walton** (1846-1928).
   Married Charles Finley McKesson.
   Children:
   > Annie Busbee McKesson (1875-1962).
   > Louis Walton McKesson.
   > Eliza McKesson McNeil.

Margaret McDowell McKesson Davis (1882-1958).

Carl McKesson (1884-1903).

Mabel McKesson (1885-1896).

Florence Matilda McKesson (1889-1963).

6. **George Walton, M.D.** (1849-1904).
Educated at Davidson College; graduated from medical school at
New York University in 1873 and moved to Illinois.
Married Annie Sheehan Johnson.
Children:

> Loretta Walton (died in infancy).
>
> Thomas George Walton.
>
> Ellen Teresa Walton.

7. **Lucy Walton** (1851-1922).
Married Reverend Neilson Falls.
Children:

> Matilda Falls (1872-1920).
>
> Lucy Walton Falls Green (1874-1914).
>
> George Walton Falls (1877-1912).
>
> Margaret Walton Falls (d. 1941).
>
> Augusta Falls Spurgin (b. 1883).
>
> Claire Falls Barry.
>
> Neilson ("Buck") Falls (1891-1957).

8. **Martha Matilda Walton** (1852-1936).
Married Charles Stuart Smith (1847-1915).
Children:

> Kathleen Walton Smith Black (1879-).
>
> William Walton Smith (1884-1964).
>
> Thomas Walton Smith (1886-1888).
>
> Carlotta Smith Norton (d. 1957)
>
> Mary Southerland Smith Sinclair (1889-1969).

9. **Florence Louise Walton (1855-1930).**
   Married John Henry Pearson (1852-1954).
   Children:
   > Jane Sophronia ("Janie") Pearson (1880-1965).
   > Clifton Walton Pearson (1881-1939).
   > Florence Walton Pearson White (1885-1971).
   > John Henry Pearson, Jr. (1886-1862).
   > Lucille Pearson (1888-1971).
   > Marie Louise Pearson (1889-1977).
   > Eliza Murphy Pearson (1892-1944).
   > Cameron Walton Pearson Poland (1898-1998).

10. **Hugh Collett Walton** (1858-1867).

11. **Herbert Huske Walton** (1860-1949).
    Married Lola Kirkland (1861-1891).
    > Children: Samuel Kirkland Walton (1889-1891).
    Married Evelyn Erwin (1879-1897).
    Married Clara Cheesborough (1860-1935).
    > Children: Louisa Anne Cheesborough Walton
    > (1899-1991). (Named later changed to Louise).
    > Married Harry Ariail Boggs (1891-1957).
    > Children:
    > > Clara Katherine Boggs Glaze (1929-).
    > > Herbert ("Sonny") Walton Boggs (1930-1992).
    > > Mary Murphy Boggs Alexander (1932-)
    > > Marie "Ariail" Boggs Wood (1934-1996).
    > > Eliza Cheesborough Boggs Kirk (1937-).
    > > Florence Septima Boggs Smith (1939-).

REFERENCES

Adams, M.B. (1995). Family connections along the Blue Ridge: The ancestry and close descendants of Margaret Erwin McDowell and James Thomas Walton. The Country Press, Inc.: Middleborough, Massachusetts.

Adams, M.B. (2000). *Old burke county relatives*. Privately published.

Bell, W.M. (1916). *The North Carolina flood: July 14, 15, 16, 1916*. W.M. Bell: Charlotte, N.C. D.H. Ramsey Library. University of North Carolina at Asheville. Special Collections and University Archives: GB1399.4.N8 N67 1916.

Benjamin, A. (1830).*The architect, or practical house carpenter*. Original publisher unknown. Subsequent reprints by L. Coffin, Boston (1844), and Benjamin B. Mussey & Company, Boston (1850).

Boggs, L.C.W. (1965). *Tales of Creekside: Historical and Supernatural*. Unpublished papers of Louise Cheesborough Walton Boggs (1899-1991).

Bott, D. (1997). Amazing Grace: A History of Grace Episcopal Church, Morganton, North Carolina and of the Missions of Burke County 1845-1995. Grace Episcopal Church: Morganton, N.C.

Charleston Earthquake, 1886. University of South Carolina. University Libraries Digital Collections. Columbia, S.C. Retrieved on May 15, 2013 from **http://library.sc.edu/digital/collections/quake.html**.

Charleston Earthquake of 1886. University of South Carolina Seismology: University of South Carolina. Department of Earth and Ocean Sciences. Retrieved on May 13, 2013 from **http://www.seis.sc.edu/projects/SCSN/history/html/eqchas.html**.

Clark, W. (1901). Histories of the several regiments and battalions from North Carolina, in the great war 1861-65. Vol 4. E.M. Uzzell: Raleigh, North Carolina.

Cotton, J.R.& Wylie, S.P. Barbee, M.M. (ed.). (1987). *Historic Burke: An Architectural Inventory of Burke County, North Carolina.* Historic Burke Foundation, Inc. Morganton, N.C.

Eliza Murphy Walton Letters, 1861-1863. Collection Number: 02686-z. Southern Historical Collection. Wilson Library. University of North Carolina at Chapel Hill. Chapel Hill, N.C.

"First Presbyterian Church." Burke County North Carolina Cemeteries. Cemetery Census: Cemetery Records on the Web. Retrieved on April 3, 2013-May 31, 2013 from **http://cemeterycensus.com/nc/burk/cem074.htm**.

"Forest Hill Cemetery." Burke County North Carolina Cemeteries. Cemetery Census: Cemetery Records on the Web. Retrieved on April 3, 2013-May 31, 2013 from **http://cemeterycensus.com/nc/burk/cem076.htm**.

Furr, M.L.A. (2013). "Willow Hill Revisited." Unpublished papers of Mary Lou Avery Furr. Morganton, NC.

"Grace Episcopal Church." Burke County North Carolina Cemeteries. Cemetery Census: Cemetery Records on the Web. Retrieved on April 3, 2013-May 31, 2013 from **http://cemeterycensus.com/nc/burk/cem090.htm**.

"Historic and Architectural Resources of Morganton." (1987). National Register of Historic Places Inventory. United States Department of the Interior. National Park Service. Retrieved on May 12, 2013 from **http://www.hpo.ncdcr.gov/nr/BK0392.pdf**.

Historic Earthquakes: Charleston, South Carolina. Retrieved on May 26, 2013 from **http://earthquake.usgs.gov/earthquakes/states/events/1886_ 09_01.php**. United States Geological Survey. United States Department of the Interior.

Holloway, J.E., Ph.D. (2009). African Crops and Slave Cuisines. Retrieved on April 5, 2013 from **http://www.history.com/topics/slavery**.

Iobst, R.W. &L.H. Manarin (1965).*The bloody sixth: The sixth north carolina regiment, confederate states of America*. North Carolina Centennial Confederate Commission. Raleigh, N.C.

John Murphy Walton Diary, 1864. Collection Number: 02695-z. Southern Historical Collection. Wilson Library. University of North Carolina at Chapel Hill. Chapel Hill, N.C.

Jones, H. G. (1973). "Magnolia Place." National Register of Historic Places Inventory. United States Department of the Interior. National Park Service. Retrieved on May 12, 2013 from **http://www.hpo.ncdcr.gov/nr/BK0007.pdf**.

Kerns, W.L., PhD. (2005). Waltons of Old Virginia and Sketches of Families of Central Virginia. Heritage Books, Inc.: Arlington, VA.

Kickler, T.L. (2013) Antebellum Gold Mining (1820-1860). North Carolina History Project. John Locke Foundation. Retrieved on June 17, 2013 from **http://www.northcarolinahistory.org/commentary/59/entry**.

Leslie, .L. (2008). "Flood of 1916 changed Biltmore Village and family lives forever." Retrieved on April 4, 2013 from **http://www.asheville.com/news/flood1916.html**. Asheville.com community news.

Manarin, L.H., comp. (1968). *North Carolina troops 1861-1865: A roster. Vol. II: Cavalry.* State Department of Archives and History: Raleigh, N.C.

Manarin, L.H., comp. (1968). *North Carolina troops 1861-1865: A roster. Vols. III & IV: Infantry.* State Department of Archives and History: Raleigh, N.C.

McCown, H. (2006). "December 1804: The Walton War." From "This Month in North Carolina History Archives." Wilson Library. University of North Carolina at Chapel Hill, N.C. Retrieved on May 12, 2013 from **http://www.lib.unc.edu/ncc/ref/nchistory/dec2006/**.

McPherson, J.M. (1988). *Battle cry of freedom: The civil war era.* Oxford University Press. New York, N.Y.

Mintzer, D. E. (1984). "Mountain View." National Register of Historic Places Inventory. United States Department of the Interior. National Park Service. Retrieved on May 12, 2013 from **http://www.hpo.ncdcr.gov/nr/BK0016.pdf**

Mull, J.A. (1975). *Tales of Old Burke.* The News Herald Press: Morganton, N.C.

North Carolina Civil War: Stoneman's Raid. Retrieved on April 20, 2013 from **http://www.civilwartraveler.com/EAST/NC/StonemansRaid. html.**

Nummer, B.A., PhD. (May 2000). "Historical Origins of Food Preservation." National Center for Home Food Preservation. Retrieved on March 10, 2013 from **http://nchfp.uga.edu/publications/nchfp/factsheets/food_pr es_hist.html.**

Osment, T.N. (2008). "Floods of 1916 and 1940." Retrieved on April 4, 2013 from **http://digitalheritage.org/2010/08/floods-of-1916-and-1940/**. The Digital Heritage Project: The Mountain Heritage Center, Western Carolina University.

Phifer, E.W., Jr. (1979). *Burke: The history of a North Carolina County, 1777-1920*. North Carolina Department of Cultural Resources. Raleigh, N.C.

Spencer, C.P. (1866). The Last Ninety Days of the War in North Carolina. Watchman Publishing Company: New York.

Schipper, M. & Stampp, K.M. (1991). Records of ante-bellum southern plantations from the revolution through the civil war. Series J, Part 7: Alabama. Southern Historical Collection, Manuscripts Department, Library of the University of North Carolina at Chapel Hill. Retrieved on June 28, 2013 from **http://www.lexisnexis.com/documents/academic/upa_cis/24 53_AnteBellSouthPlanSerJPt7.pdf**

Schipper, M. & Stampp, K.M. (1992). Records of ante-bellum southern plantations from the revolution through the civil war. Series J, Part 14: Western North Carolina. Southern Historical Collection, Manuscripts Department, Library of the University of North Carolina at Chapel Hill. Retrieved on June 28, 2013 from **http://www.lexisnexis.com/documents/academic/upa_cis/24 53_AnteBellSouthPlanSerJPt14.pdf**

The Burke County Historical Society. (1981). *Burke County Heritage: North Carolina*. Vols I &II, Morganton, North Carolina. Hunter Publishing: Winston-Salem, N.C.

Thomas George Walton Papers, 1779-1897. Collection Number: 00748. Southern Historical Collection. Wilson Library. University of North Carolina at Chapel Hill. Chapel Hill, N.C.

U.S. Military Historical Records by War: Civil War Collections. Retrieved on April24-May 6, 2013 from **http://www.fold3.com/**.

Walton, T. G. (1865). Amnesty Petition, July 13, 1865. Case files of applications from former confederates for presidential pardons ("Amnesty Papers"), 1865-67. Records of the Adjutant General's Office, 1780s-1917, Record Group 94, Publication M1003, National Archives, Washington, D.C.

Walton, T.G. Letters of Colonel Thomas George Walton (1814-1905). Property of family.

Walton, T.G., Colonel (1984). *Sketches of the pioneers in Burke County history.* Southern Historical Press, Inc.: Greenville, SC.

Watford, C.M. (ed). (2003). *The civil war in North Carolina: Soldiers' and civilians' letters and diaries, 1861-1865.* Volume 2: The mountains. McFarland & Company, Inc. Jefferson, N.C.

Watterman, T. T. & Johnston, F.B. (1947). *The early architecture of North Carolina.* The University of North Carolina Press: Chapel Hill, NC.

Weber, M. (1981). The civil war concentration camps. 2013 Institute for Historical Review. *The Journal of Historical Review.* Summer, 1981. Vol. 2, No. 2, 137. Retrieved on June 9, 2013 from **http://www.ihr.org/jhr/v02/v02p137_Weber.html**.

Wells, J. B. III. (1969). "Creekside." National Register of Historic Places Inventory. United States Department of the Interior, National Park Service. Retrieved on May 12, 2013 from **http://www.hpo.ncdcr.gov/nr/BK0004.pdf**.

www.ingramcontent.com/pod-product-compliance
Lightning Source LLC
LaVergne TN
LVHW011224080426
835509LV00005B/315